Classic Pentecostal Sermon Library

Classic Pentecostal Sermon Library

Ray H. Hughes Sr.

Volume 4

Pathway Press

All Scripture quotations, unless otherwise noted, are taken from the King James Version of the Bible.

Scripture quotations marked Amp. are taken from *The Amplified Bible*, New Testament. Copyright © 1954, 1958, 1987, by The Lockman Foundation. Used by permission.

Editorial Staff: Lance Colkmire, Tom George, Tammy Hatfield, and Esther Metaxas

Edited by Tom George

Cover design and graphics by Mark Shuler
Inside pages design by Tom George

Library of Congress Control Number: 2011920087
ISBN: 9781596845640, hardcover edition
ISBN: 9781596845657, softcover edition

P

1080 Montgomery Avenue
Cleveland, Tennessee 37311

Visit *www.pathwaypress.org* for more information.

Printed in the United States of America

DEDICATION

This series of sermons is dedicated to the many thousands of people—both clergy and laity—that make up the faithful "cloud of witnesses" who over the past seventy years have mentored and encouraged me, undergirded me with their prayers, and supported my ministry—first as a teenage preacher and throughout the years in the many places the Lord has privileged me to serve Him and His Church. ✞

CONTENTS

FOREWORD

My heroes have always been preachers. At the top of that list—second only to my father—has been Dr. Ray H. Hughes Sr. For more than seventy years, Dr. Hughes has shaken the foundations of hell and rescued thousands of souls from eternal destruction. Perhaps no other preacher of his time has so passionately pursued the lost and confronted the powers of darkness. His messages on the baptism in the Holy Spirit have led multitudes into the Spirit-filled life and given leadership to a movement that now encompasses more than 650 million people worldwide. He is a man of uncompromised conviction and unprecedented anointing.

On November 27, 1983, while serving as president of Lee College (now Lee University), Dr. Hughes preached a message on the cross of Jesus Christ titled "The Meaning of Calvary." The Holy Spirit brought the vicarious sufferings of Jesus home to my heart that day. I saw the Cross. I saw my life. I saw a world that was lost. Through tears and heavy travail, I accepted the call to preach the gospel.

Now, in his "Caleb" years, Dr. Hughes seeks to impart many of his sermons to a new generation of ministers and laity. This fourth volume of the *Classic Pentecostal Sermon Library* contains manuscripts from a God-called evangelist. To those of us who have come under his influence, these writings are treasures of his legacy. To those who are new to his ministry, these writings will give you glimpses into a heart fully surrendered to the Great Commission.

John Wesley said:

> Give me one hundred preachers who fear nothing but sin, and desire nothing but God, and I care not a straw whether they be clergymen or laymen; such alone will shake the gates of hell and set up the kingdom of heaven on earth.

Dr. Ray H. Hughes Sr. has been such a man.

May God raise up a new generation of men and women who will hear and heed His call to preach the gospel of Jesus Christ in the Spirit and power of Pentecost.

—Mark L. Williams
Assistant General Overseer
Church of God

ACKNOWLEDGMENTS

This sermon series was conceived in the heart of the Reverend David Ray, Pathway Press administrative assistant. I deeply appreciate Brother Ray's interest in making this work available to ministers, teachers, and lay workers.

Reverend Terry Hart, director of publications, has been very supportive in bringing this material to publication.

Dr. Tom George, editor of the *Classic Pentecostal Sermon Library*, has assisted me greatly in preparing this material for publication.

I would be remiss if I failed to acknowledge the many people who have contributed to my life and ministry during the past seventy years and thus have had a hand in bringing this project to its present stage.

I take this opportunity to acknowledge the hand of God upon my life, and I pray that those who read this series will experience some of the same anointing that I experienced in delivering these messages.

Those who read these sermons can now complement my ministry by continuing to proclaim throughout the world the good news of the gospel.

INTRODUCTION

For some time, I have had a strong yearning to leave a legacy for younger ministers and Christian workers who will come after me. I am aware that I am "set for the defence of the gospel" (Phil. 1:17), and I have a great desire for the church to continue in "the faith which was once delivered unto the saints" (Jude 3).

It is my observation that doctrines, practices, and worthy traditions are soon lost, and many people have no guiding star to point them to the wonderful treasure of truth found in the Word of God.

It was for this reason that I was delighted when David Ray of Pathway Press approached me with a proposal to include these works from my extensive files in a project called *Classic Pentecostal Sermon Library*. I am honored to have been chosen as a contributor to this series, which I believe will become an important resource for our ministers, teachers, and lay workers.

Throughout my more than seventy years of ministry, I have endeavored to preach the Word, and my sermons will reflect this commitment. This series is categorized as evangelistic, doctrinal, revival, prophecy, special occasions, and devotional and are listed for easy reference.

These sermons are textual messages, with numbered divisions and many Scripture references, so that a busy Christian worker has a resource at his fingertips. Hopefully, as well as material for ministry, readers also will find this series to be inspirational devotional reading, enriching one's appreciation of the precious Word of God, which is the foundation of our faith and our guide for Christian living.

It is with deep appreciation for the hand of God upon my life and ministry that I now pass on this legacy of resources to my fellow ministers and lay workers with the full understanding that "all scripture is given by inspiration of God, and is profitable for doctrine, for reproof, for correction, for instruction in righteousness: that the man of God may be perfect, throughly furnished unto all good works" (2 Tim. 3:16-17). ✞

DR. RAY H. HUGHES SR.

ABOUT THE AUTHOR

Dr. Ray H. Hughes Sr. is a Georgia native, born March 7, 1924, in Calhoun. He began his ministry January 1, 1940, was first licensed by the Church of God in 1941, and was ordained to the church's highest rank of ministry in 1950.

After several years of successful evangelistic ministry, Dr. Hughes pastored churches at Fairfield, Illinois, 1945-46;

and North Chattanooga, Tennessee, 1948-52. Following a very fruitful pastorate at North Chattanooga, he was chosen by the church to serve as general director of Youth and Christian Education, 1952-56.

Dr. Hughes was appointed to serve as state overseer of Maryland-Delaware-DC at the 1956 General Assembly. He served there until 1960, when he was appointed president of Lee College, serving there until 1966. During his tenure at Lee College, Dr. Hughes also served as national radio speaker for *Forward in Faith*, 1960-63.

In 1966, Dr. Hughes began a long history of service in the highest elected general leadership positions of the Church of God: third assistant general overseer, 1966-68, 1992-94; second assistant general overseer, 1968-70; first assistant general overseer, 1970-72, 1976-78, 1986-90, 1994-96; general overseer, 1972-74, 1978-82, 1996.

Dr. Hughes also served on the Church of God Executive Council, 1956-60, 1962-82, 1986-90, 1992-96, and 1998-2002.

In addition to his many elected leadership positions, Dr. Hughes also has served in the following appointed leadership positions: director, General Board of Education; National Sunday School and Youth Board; president, Lee College, 1960-66, 1982-84; president, Church of God School of Theology, 1984-86; and chairman, Evangelism and Home Missions Board.

Areas where Dr. Hughes served as state overseer were Delaware-Maryland-DC, 1956-60, and Georgia, 1974-76.

From 1990 to 1992, Dr. Hughes served the church as a national evangelist. He also served on the evangelistic field for nine years during his early ministry.

Dr. Hughes' educational accomplishments include Lee College, A.A., D.Litt; Tennessee Wesleyan College, B.A.; University of Tennessee, M.S., Ed.D.

Interdenominationly, Dr. Hughes has served as president, National Association of Evangelicals (NAE), 1986-88; NAE Executive Committee, 1978-89; permanent member of the NAE Board of Administration; chairman, Pentecostal Fellowship of North America (PFNA), 1976-78; PCCNA Advisory Council member; National Sunday School Association member; chairman, Pentecostal World Conference, 1989-98; vice chairman, Pentecostal World Conference, 1978-89; Pentecostal World Conference Presidium and Advisory Committee member; and Pentecostal World Conference speaker.

Dr. Hughes' honors and recognitions include Hall of Prophets, Church of God Theological Seminary; Who's Who in Education; Who's Who in America; Pi Delta Omicron; and Phi Delta Kappa.

A prolific writer, Dr. Hughes' many published books include *The Rapture and Revelation*; *The Cross, Love's Necessity*; *Lord, Show Us Thy Glory*; *The Order of Future Events*; *Religion on Fire*; *Planning for Sunday School Progress*; *What Is Pentecost?*; *The Effect of Lee College on World Missions*; *The Outpouring of the Spirit*; *State Overseers' Manual*; *The Transition of Church-Related Junior Colleges to Senior Colleges*; *Pentecostal Preaching*; *Who Is the Holy Ghost?*; *Church of God Distinctives*; and *Dynamics of Sunday School Growth.* ✞

AS IT WAS IN THE DAYS OF NOAH AND LOT

"As it was in the days of Noe, so shall it be also in the days of the Son of man. They did eat, they drank, they married wives, they were given in marriage, until the day that Noe entered into the ark, and the flood came, and destroyed them all. Likewise also as it was in the days of Lot; they did eat, they drank, they bought, they sold, they planted, they builded; but the same day that Lot went out of Sodom it rained fire and brimstone from heaven, and destroyed them all. Even thus shall it be in the day when the Son of man is revealed"
(Luke 17:26-30).

INTRODUCTION

There is a striking similarity between the days of Noah and Lot and these modern times. Jesus told His disciples that when conditions prevail as they did in the days of Lot, and during the period before the flood, it is an indication that we are approaching the end of the age and the coming of the Son of man. When one reads the Book of Genesis and compares it with the sins of our day, he must marvel at the precision with which Christ describes our day by saying, "As it was . . . so shall it be" (Luke 17:26). In the days of Lot and Noah there was almost a full rejection of God. For several decades Noah preached righteousness to his generation, but was only able to convince seven others of the righteousness of God. The Word of God says, "And spared not the old world, but saved Noah the eighth person, a preacher of righteousness, bringing in the flood upon the world of the ungodly" (2 Peter 2:5). And, in 1 Peter 3:20: "Which sometime were disobedient, when once the longsuffering of God waited in the days of Noah, while the ark was a preparing, wherein few, that is, eight souls were saved by water." Noah was an upright man who found favor in the eyes of God, but men would not heed his message of righteousness.

The same was true in the days of Lot. When Lot's uncle Abraham prayed for his safekeeping and asked God if he would spare Sodom and Gomorrah if there were ten righteous in the city, God promised that He would. After he had ceased his prayer he looked toward Sodom and Gomorrah and saw them burning as a furnace afire, for there were only three righteous who escaped the judgment of God, Lot and his two daughters.

This is evidence, my friend, that the population before the flood and during the days of Lot had almost totally rejected God. God was not in all of their thoughts.

I. OVERINDULGENCE

Another condition in the days of Noah and Lot set forth by the Lord Jesus Christ was eating and drinking. Now there is nothing wrong with eating and drinking; they are both necessary for the existence of the human race. But this eating has reference to surfeiting, overindulgence, living to satisfy the sensual appetite. The apostle Paul properly described this sort of people by saying, "Whose God is their belly, and whose glory is in their shame" (Phil. 3:19). Jesus warned us against making the satisfaction of the physical man the main purpose and object of life: "And take heed to yourselves, lest at any time your hearts be overcharged with surfeiting, and drunkenness, and cares of this life, and so that day come upon you unawares. For as a snare shall it come on all them that dwell on the face of the whole earth" (Luke 21:34-35).

Jesus said that they would not only be eating, but drinking. This no doubt has reference to drunkenness. Drink has become so prominent that one is considered almost a social outcast if he does not participate. Social pressure is brought to bear upon people in our generation until they feel as though they are not a part of society unless they drink. Businessmen feel that they must take a social drink in order to maintain their businesses.

II. SEXUAL SINS

Another condition set forth by Christ is that they married wives. Matthew explains it like this: "They were . . . marrying and giving in marriage" (24:38). In that day the idea that one man should be married to one woman was tabooed. Even Lamech, Noah's father, "took unto him two wives" (Gen. 4:19). Marriage had become a mere convenience for the satisfaction of lustful desires, and men married for lust and not for love. Marriage bonds were snapped at the least provocation and the sacredness and sanctity of this whole union was no longer considered in the light of God's commands. This all comes from a warped idea of marriage and disregard for the commands of God. A man should be the husband of one wife.

We are not only faced with marriages and divorces, the sin of infidelity and adultery, but also the prominence of one of the most horrid, disgusting sins of all times–the sin of sodomy, or homosexuality. Jude states that this was prominent in the days of Lot: "Even as Sodom and Gomorrha, and the cities about them in like manner, giving themselves over to fornication, and going after strange flesh, are set forth for an example, suffering the vengeance of eternal fire" (v. 7). Read the horrible story for yourself in Genesis 19.

The cry of wickedness, immorality, and violence was so great that the Bible says "the men of Sodom were wicked and sinners before the Lord exceedingly" (13:13). "And the Lord said, Because the cry of Sodom and Gomorrah is great, and because their sin is very grievous; I will go down now, and see whether they have done altogether according to the cry of it, which is come unto me; and if not, I will know" (18:20-21).

In Genesis 19, it is revealed that God sent two angels to Sodom. Out of that large city there was only one place for them to lodge because there was only one righteous, believing family in the whole city of Sodom, and that was Lot's family. But a portion of that family had already been tainted by the sins of Sodom. The men of the town heard that the visitors were being entertained by Lot: "But before they lay down, the men of the city, even the men of Sodom, compassed the house round, both old and young, all the people from every quarter: and they called unto Lot, and said unto him, Where are the men which came in to thee this night? bring them out unto us, that we may know them" (vv. 4-5). Here is where this horrible sin received its name—*sodomy*. Here is the first biblical mention or record of this debasing crime. Sodom had so deteriorated that this was a common sin, not only of the old but young men as well. This is the thing that happens when man begins to worship the creatures instead of the Creator.

The Word of God does not adopt a hush-hush attitude toward this subject but is very plain in its denunciation of it: "For this cause God gave them up unto vile affections: for even their women did change the natural use into that which is against nature: and likewise also the men, leaving the natural use of the woman, burned in their lust one toward another; men with men working that which is unseemly, and receiving in themselves that recompense of their error which was meet" (Rom. 1:26-27). The sin that has caused the public to bow their heads in shame is prominent in government circles, in the schools and universities, in community gangs and clubs, and in special organized societies. Men burning in their own lust are seeking satisfaction for their fitful nature. I am aware that this is a horrible picture to paint, but nevertheless it is true.

We must not close our eyes to the fact that the Bible says, "And as it was in the days of Noe, so shall it be also in the days of the Son of man" (Luke 17:26). These things existed in those days, and today they exist in even a more pronounced manner than most of us are aware. The warped idea of sex has so completely possessed this generation until it oozes from the pores of American life. The pornographic literature that is now published under the guise of art is used to inflame the passions of its readers. The reason this business has continued to grow is because of public demand for such filth. These filth factories are grinding out this garbage for the consumption of the young people in our generation, which means that unless God gives us a revival our future is damned.

III. FILTHY CONVERSATION

Another condition of the days of Lot is revealed in 2 Peter 2:7: "And delivered just Lot, vexed with the filthy conversation of the wicked." Filthy conversation was common in the days of Lot. Today the air reeks with profanity, filthy jokes, and filthy conversations. One can hardly engage in a conversation with the average man without being subjected to this wickedness. This reveals the depravity of the human heart.

The Bible says, "For as he thinketh in his heart, so is he" (Prov. 23:7). This was the condition of the days of Noah: "And God saw that the wickedness of man was great in the earth, and that every imagination of the thoughts of his heart was only evil continually" (Gen. 6:5).

The days of Noah and Lot were times of material achievements. The Bible says, "They bought, they sold, they planted, they builded" (Luke 17:28). Christ is setting forth here that materialism dominated that day. Likewise, men have become so materialistic in our times until they have not time for Almighty God.

CONCLUSION

The Word of God warns us about becoming so engrossed in these times and so busy with the cares of this life that that day will overtake us unawares: "For in such an hour as ye think not the Son of man cometh" (Matt. 24:44). He will come "as a thief in the night" (1 Thess. 5:2). He will come suddenly—"in a moment, in the twinkling of an eye" (1 Cor. 15:52).

The masses of the world will not realize it until it is too late. The antediluvians were not made aware of the importance of the preaching of righteousness until Noah was safe in the ark "and the Lord shut him in" (Gen. 7:16). The Sodomites would not heed the warnings of righteousness and committed gross immoralities until the very day that God destroyed the cities of the plains with fire and brimstone.

Accept my warning that the day of Christ is at hand. All of these signs and indications of the last days are what Jesus meant when He said, "And as it was in the days of Noe, so shall it be also in the days of the Son of man" (Luke 17:26). Are you prepared to meet God at this moment? Bow your head right where you are and repent of your sins and ask Jesus to save you. ✠

BLESSED ASSURANCE

"I know whom I have believed, and am persuaded that he is able to keep that which I have committed unto him against that day" (2 Tim. 1:12).

INTRODUCTION

Man is a spiritual being as well as a physical being and his spirit searches after the supernatural. In his search for security, he has come to believe in many things and adhere to many religious practices. The world is religious but religiously lost. It is possible for one to be zealous and devout about a religion and yet be lost. The wise man Solomon said, "There is a way which seemeth right unto a man, but the end thereof are the ways of death" (Prov. 14:12). There is so much truth mixed with error and so many religions that please the carnal senses of men, but these ways which seem right can lead one to death.

A few years ago, while attending a convention in Haiti, I was invited by a leading doctor of the city to attend a voodoo service. For five hours until 3:30 in the morning, I sat awestricken by the heathen dances and ceremonies. Musicians beat out weird tunes on the tom-toms, while a group of women dressed in white chanted in weird monotones, offered a sacrifice of fowls, and went through rituals. Toward the closing of their ceremony, they began to pray to different things. I was told by one of our group that many of these people would attend an early church service that morning. All of this discontentment and unrest was because they had not found assurance and they were seeking after security. Their spirit was crying out for something that would bring lasting peace to their lives. This was the thing that Paul detected when he went to Athens and beheld the superstitions of the Athenians as he stood in the midst of Mars Hill and saw there an altar with the inscription TO THE UNKNOWN GOD. The city of Athens was wholly given to idolatry and they worshipped thousands of Gods. Yet, they had not found the assurance for which the human heart longs. Therefore an altar was erected to the unknown god.

I. GOD WANTS YOU TO BE ASSURED OF YOUR SALVATION

Today, you can have positive assurance through Jesus Christ our Lord. You can have assurance that Christ is real in your heart by faith. You have a right to know and when it comes to eternal things, God wants you to know. You can say with the apostle Paul, "I know whom I have believed, and am persuaded that he is able to keep that which I have committed unto him against that day" (2 Tim. 1:12). He spoke with authority and certainty. He knew the time and the place where his sins were washed away. He knew the day he had met the Lord and there was no guesswork about it. Paul had a personal encounter with Jesus Christ. He had met the Lord; he had been introduced to Him. He had heard the voice of the Lord and had seen His glory and could not doubt his experience. Therefore he was able to say, "I know whom I have believed" (v. 12). He did not merely know Jesus Christ historically, but he knew Him experientially.

Many of the religions of the world are known only traditionally, and many Christians are Christians only in tradition. But

Paul could testify that he had experienced "the excellency of the knowledge of Christ Jesus my Lord" (Phil. 3:8). So many people who profess Christianity have to confess that they do not know what a change of heart means or what it means to be born again, or to be born from above. They have never undergone this change. Their religion is mere outward ritual and ceremony; there has not been a change in their lives. But God did not leave His people in doubt, and we do not have to wait until the resurrection of the body or the coming of the Lord Jesus Christ to have this assurance. We can have this assurance in this life, as well as the life that is to come.

II. THE ASSURANCE OF SALVATION IS FOUND IN JESUS

It has been said that he who knows not and knows not that he knows not is a fool–instruct him. He who knows and knows not that he knows is asleep–awaken him. He who knows and knows that he knows is wise–follow him. True religion is reposed in a person. The apostle Paul said, "I know whom I have believed." Not necessarily *what* we have believed, but *whom* we have believed–"In whom we have redemption through his blood, the forgiveness of sins" (Eph. 1:7). So assurance comes, not through intellectual assent, but through a personal attachment to Jesus Christ. It is impossible for one to go through the birth pains of the new birth without knowing it.

You can part with uncertainty today, for the great assurance of salvation is yours. The world is filled with professors of religion. The formal churches stage campaigns to fill their church rolls with unregenerate souls until the church itself has become one of the greatest fields of evangelism in all the world. People are joining the church to ease their conscience. The church has become a mere convenience rather than the center of true life. The Bible says, "Professing themselves to be wise, they became fools" (Rom. 1:22). Some minister has told them they are saved. They have made a profession but their fruits deny their possession. The Bible says, "By their fruits ye shall know them" (Matt. 7:20). And if others shall know them, certainly they can know themselves. The majority of church members who go through the motion of religion in our day are lost. I don't have much confidence in a religion without the prerequisites of salvation—conviction, repentance, and confession. Any experience outside of this true experience is superficial and is not founded upon the Word of God. It is mere intellectual conception and not a genuine experience.

One of the greatest curses to Christianity today is those professors who are occupied with the doctrine and not with the practice. They profess to know Him but in their works they deny Him. God's Word says, "If any man among you seem to be religious, and bridleth not his tongue, but deceiveth his own heart, this man's religion is vain" (James 1:26). Notice that this scripture says a man can seem to be religious and yet his own experience be vain. This is what Jesus said to the Pharisees. They went through the form of religion, paid their tithes, fasted twice a week, would not eat out of unwashed vessels, kept the Sabbath, believed in angels, spirits, and the resurrection, yet Jesus called them hypocrites. James said, "But be ye doers of the word, and not hearers only, deceiving your own selves" (v. 22). How many thousands of religionists deceive themselves every day?

The Bible says, "For if a man think himself to be something, when he is nothing, he deceiveth himself" (Gal. 6:3). Most people have heard of the right way but they will not give heed to the way. In most cases it is not a matter of hearing more about Christ, it's a matter of putting into practice what we have already heard about Him. If you do not have the assurance of Jesus Christ in your heart, I want to help you today.

III. GOD'S WORD GIVES US THE ASSURANCE OF SALVATION

In the first epistle of John, the frequent recurrence of the word *know* throughout the five chapters of this book is evidence to me that God wants everyone to have the assurance of salvation. If you will read these five chapters carefully, you can know Jesus Christ as your personal Savior. One cannot read too long in any one place in this epistle without coming across the word *know*. This epistle is filled with experiential knowledge of the Lord Jesus Christ.

John begins by saying, "That which was from the beginning, which we have heard, which we have seen with our eyes, which we have looked upon, and our hands have handled, of the Word of life" (1 John 1:1). John says the reason that I can write with such assurance and make the declaration that I am making is that I heard Him, I saw Him, I looked upon Him and beheld His glory, and my hands touched Him. I know Him. I know Him from the standpoint of His Word because I have heard Him. I know Him from the standpoint of His example because I have seen Him. I know Him from the standpoint of spiritual perception because I have beheld Him. I know Him from the standpoint of the senses because I have touched Him. John's experience was built upon a personal attachment to the Lord Jesus Christ.

The apostle Peter said, "Whom having not seen, ye love; in whom, though now ye see him not, yet believing, ye rejoice with joy unspeakable and full of glory" (1 Peter 1:8). There is a joy, an ecstasy, and a glory that accompanies the experience of salvation, an indescribable peace and certainty that all believers can and should experience. When one has this experience there is warmth that comes into his soul. Then he realizes that religion is not just something that goes on round about him, or something of an external nature, but it is something that goes down inside him. Regardless of what happens in his environs, it need not disturb his heart.

Here are some scriptures of assurance:

"And hereby we do know that we know him, if we keep his commandments" (1 John 2:3). We can be assured that we know the Lord Jesus Christ if our knowledge of Him constrains us to keep His commandments. Those who keep His Word have the assurance of His presence. This is knowledge by obedience, for the Scripture says, "He that saith, I know him, and keepeth not his commandments, is a liar, and the truth is not in him" (v. 4). This is very plain language, my friend, but I think we can all understand it, for "he that saith he abideth in him ought himself also so to walk, even as he walked" (v. 6). Those who profess to abide with Him must walk with Him after His pattern and example. If one is not obedient to His Word, it is evident that the Word is not in his heart.

Our next scripture of assurance is found in verse 14: "We know that we have passed from death unto life, because we love the brethren. He that loveth not his brother abideth in death." Then 1 John 4:7-8 says, "Beloved, let us love one another: for love is of God; and every one that loveth is born of God, and knoweth God. He that loveth not knoweth not God; for God is love." Love is the heart, the nucleus, the center of old-time religion. "If a man say, I love God, and hateth his brother, he is a liar: for he that loveth not his brother whom he hath seen, how can he love God whom he hath not seen?" (v. 20). Love is a measuring stick of your Christian experience and without love, man is lost. Love is the manifestation by which the entire world can know that you are a Christian. "By this shall all men know that ye are my disciples, if ye have love one to another" (John 13:35). And the Bible says that love is the mark of assurance of true Christianity: "And hereby we know that we are of the truth, and shall assure our hearts before him" (1 John 3:19).

The third scripture of assurance is 1 John 3:24: "And hereby we know that he abideth in us, by the Spirit which he hath given us." The Holy Ghost is the agent of our experience; it is He who brings assurance to our hearts. And we know that He abides in us, because He has given of His Spirit: "Hereby know we that we dwell in him, and he in us, because he hath given us of his Spirit" (4:13). "For as many as are led by the Spirit of God, they are the sons of God" (Rom. 8:14). "He that believeth on the Son of God hath the witness in himself" (1 John 5:10).

CONCLUSION

Time will not permit me to elaborate upon all the scriptures of assurance that are found in this wonderful Book, but you can read them for yourselves. John said:

- "I have not written unto you because ye know not the truth, but because ye know it" (1 John 2:21).
- "If ye know that he is righteous, ye know that every one that doeth righteousness is born of him" (v. 29).
- "Beloved, now are we the sons of God, and it doth not yet appear what we shall be: but we know that, when he shall appear, we shall be like him; for we shall see him as he is" (3:2).
- "These things have I written unto you . . . that ye may know that ye have eternal life, and that ye may believe on the name of the Son of God" (5:13).

Oh, blessed assurance, Jesus is mine!

This little epistle is filled with assurance for everyone who desires to find security in Christ Jesus. This becomes the grand benediction, and the final verses of this book say:

> We know that whosoever is born of God sinneth not; but he that is begotten of God keepeth himself, and that wicked one toucheth him not. And we know that we are of God, and the whole world lieth in wickedness. And we

know that the Son of God is come, and hath given us an understanding, that we may know him that is true, and we are in him that is true, even in his Son Jesus Christ (1 John 5:18-20).

You can have this assurance today. Believe on the Lord Jesus Christ that you may know Him as your personal Savior. ✞

CRIES FROM THE CROSS

"Father, forgive them; for they know not what they do" (Luke 23:34);
"Verily I say unto thee, To day shalt thou be with me in paradise" (v. 43);
"Woman, behold thy son! . . . Behold thy mother!" (John 19:26-27).

INTRODUCTION

As we approach this season of our Lord's death, we are reminded that no scene in human history has such a dark background but such a bright foreground. Against the background of hate, there was a foregleam of love; against the background of tragedy, there was a forecast of triumph; against the background of sin, there was the promise of hope; against the background of cursing, we see the brightness of blessing; and against the background of the fading hopes of sorrowing disciples, we hear the prediction of a coming Kingdom.

Standing on the skull-shaped hill called Calvary, the three crosses outlined against the blue sky, one is made aware of the contrasts of this event: light amidst darkness, a rose between thorns, a lily amidst the muck and mire, a lone star shining in the darkest night, love against the backdrop of hate, peace amidst disturbance, and hope amidst hopelessness. This passion seen at Calvary opens and closes with prayer. The Word of God has recorded these seven last sayings of our dying Lord.

The dying words of a person are usually important. But more important words never were spoken than the last words of our Lord. Of these seven sayings, three are addressed to God, three to man, and the seventh calls the universe to witness. The Word of God records the sayings of over ninety living saints, but the dying statements of only three saints are recorded, other than those of the Lord Jesus Christ—the statements of Israel, Moses, and Stephen.

These cries from the cross hold for us a world full of meaning. The first three cries seem to be filled with love:

- "Father, forgive them; for they know not what they do" (Luke 23:34).
- "Verily I say unto thee, To day shalt thou be with me in paradise" (v. 43).
- "Woman, behold thy son! . . . Behold thy mother!" (John 19:26-27).

The next two cries are filled with tragedy:

- "My God, my God, why hast thou forsaken me?" (Mark 15:34).
- "I thirst" (John 19:28).

The last two cries are cries of victory:

- "It is finished" (v. 30).
- "Father, into thy hands I commend my spirit" (Luke 23:46).

The cries from the cross began with Jesus supplicating for sinners—the deathless prayer of a dying Savior for fallen man.

I. THE CRY OF LOVE: "FATHER, FORGIVE THEM"

Listen to the first cry of love: "Father, forgive them" (Luke 23:34). It is not a prayer for Himself. If there ever was a time in human history when one could have been justified to have been occupied with one's own sufferings, it was this occasion. But Jesus was not occupied with His own passion, but with lips filled with the wine of love, He cried forth, "Father, forgive them." For whom was He praying? For none other than His murderers who had committed the ghastliest deed of all human atrocities. The Bible classifies this group as dogs, wolves, and ravening lions. All about Him was a raging sea of human fury; eyes were centered upon Him through which hell was looking. Blasphemies were cast at His feet as they tore from a thousand throats. All about Him He could see faces with lines of madness, but amidst such a horrible scene He shook heaven and earth with His prayer: "Father, forgive them; for they know not what they do."

Jesus practiced what He preached. No doubt a number of those about the cross had heard Him say, "Love your enemies, bless them that curse you, do good to them that hate you, and pray for them which despitefully use you, and persecute you" (Matt. 5:44). And, no doubt, they had heard Him say, "When ye stand praying, forgive, if ye have ought against any" (Mark 11:25). He had preached to forgive without limit. What He preached on the Mount He was able to practice at Calvary. This is the picture of the grace of forgiveness in all of its perfections.

This prayer for forgiveness was the fulfillment of the prophecy of Isaiah seven hundred years prior to this time. Isaiah said, "He was numbered with the transgressors; and he bare the sin of many, and made intercession for the transgressors" (53:12). Jesus' prayer was a prayer for the blackest sinners of all history. We have the glorious consolation that His prayer was heard. On the Day of Pentecost, just fifty days after, before the excitement of Calvary had time to die, God answered this prayer of His Son, who had died on the cross, and three thousand accepted Him, some of whom were the actual murderers of the Lord Jesus. Peter charged them thus: "Ye have taken, and by wicked hands have crucified and slain" (Acts 2:23). "Therefore let all the house of Israel know assuredly, that God hath made that same Jesus, whom ye have crucified, both Lord and Christ" (v. 36). On a later occasion, the apostle drew the minds of the people back to the cross. He brought the scene of Calvary fresh before them by saying, "But ye denied the Holy One and the Just, and desired a murderer to be granted unto you; and killed the Prince of life, whom God hath raised from the dead; whereof we are witnesses" (3:14). Then he said, "And now, brethren, I wot that through ignorance ye did it, as did also your rulers" (v. 17). Then he called upon them to repent: "Repent ye therefore, and be converted, that your sins maybe blotted out" (v. 19). May the entire world today hear the words of affection, "Father, forgive them."

II. THE CRY OF FORGIVENESS: "TO DAY SHALT THOU BE WITH ME IN PARADISE"

The second cry of love from the cross was the promise to a penitent thief, who had said to Jesus, "Lord, remember me when thou comest into thy kingdom" (Luke 23:42). And Jesus said unto him, "Verily I say unto thee, To day shalt thou be with me in paradise" (v. 43). This was not a question, as some would have you believe, but it was a direct promise to a vile sinner.

On the cross, Jesus was only following the pattern that He had followed throughout His life. He came to seek and to save that which was lost. He came not to call the righteous but sinners to repentance. Christ Jesus came into the world to save sinners.

Now placed between two thieves, like a shaft of light in the midst of darkness, the Holy One of God was expiring. Notice this man to whom Christ gave the invitation to enter paradise was a thief. I see in this scene some of the greatest faith in the entire Bible. The crucified man trusting in another crucified Man. On the way to Calvary, he had heard the rattle of the crowd, he had heard the accusations against Christ, and he had heard them say, "He says He is the King of the Jews." Then the thief looked at the superscription that was written over Jesus in Greek, Latin, and Hebrew: "This is the King of the Jews" (v. 38). The thief seemed to receive light that Jesus was actually a king. The light shined into his heart and he said, "Lord, remember me when thou comest into thy kingdom" (v. 42)—as if to say, "Others might not believe You are a king, but I believe You are a king. I believe You have a kingdom and when You come into Your kingdom, don't forget me."

Notice the steps to salvation taken by this penitent thief. He confessed his sins, for he said, "We receive the due reward of our deeds" (v. 41). He confessed the deity of Christ, for he said, "This man hath done nothing amiss" (v. 41). He called Jesus "Lord" (v. 42), which was a prayer of surrender. He looked to Jesus as the Master, which made him a subject or a servant. Then came the cry "Remember me" (v. 42). And He who had practiced receiving sinners all His life could not turn from even the vilest in His dying hour, but with a thorn-pierced brow and a face stained with blotches of blood, with blood exuding from the wounds of His body, and with the weight of mankind's sins and sicknesses upon Him, He took time to say, "To day shalt thou be with me in paradise" (v. 43). Today, this same tender Lord offers to the entire human race this same expression of love and the same invitation to spend eternity with Him.

He did not tell the thief that he had to be baptized, join the church, sign a card, or shake the preacher's hand. Neither did He tell him that he must go through a purgatorial cleansing, but He said, "To day shalt thou be with me in paradise" (v. 43). The dying thief became the first one to be covered with the blood of the cross.

III. THE CRY OF CONCERN: "BEHOLD THY SON! . . . BEHOLD THY MOTHER!"

The third cry of love from the cross is set forth in these words: "When Jesus therefore saw his mother, and the disciple standing by, whom he loved, he saith unto his mother, Woman, behold thy son! Then saith he to the disciple, Behold thy mother!" (John 19:26-27). From that hour the disciple took her unto his own home. Amidst this Christ-rejecting, hate-ridden crowd was this little vein of warmth—a small company of followers—just a few devout women and John the Beloved. This group included Mary, the mother of Jesus. The third saying from the cross was directed to her and to John, His bosom disciple. Oh, what love is exemplified in His dying hour! His thoughts were upon others. He came to others, lived for others, and now He was dying for others.

I have always thought of the cross of Christ as an exhibition of love. But, in this story I see tenderness and a new love expressed that many people do not realize. I see the true unselfishness of the love of God's Son. He must take time in His dying hour even to make provision for His mother. Joseph had been dead for many years and Mary was now a widow. Christ did not forsake her. This should be comfort to all the mothers in our land, especially to those mothers who have lost their companions. Jesus, in His infinite love, will take care of you. He'll take care of your children. He'll make provision for you. Life to Mary had been one continual mystery from the time the angel Gabriel made the announcement that she should bring forth a son, even though she had never known a man, until the time that Jesus was found in the Temple at the age of twelve questioning the doctors of the law and answering the difficult questions, until the day that He raised the dead, healed the sick, and opened the eyes of the blind, and until now when she saw the innocent and pure One undergoing excruciating pain. She still could not understand. To give His mother courage in the darkest hour of His life, He appointed a guardian for her. Here I see love at its height; I see love and grace in its perfection. For many years, Mary had pondered in her heart the words of Simeon when Jesus was only eight days old: "Yea, a sword shall pierce through thy own soul also" (Luke 2:35). The prophecy had now come true. A sword was piercing the heart of Mary.

The shadow of the Cross had hung over His cradle. The shadow of the Cross had followed Him through His life, but now Mary stands with pale face and throbbing heart as the mockery of the crowd lacerates her soul, while her son, evidently her only source of support, is expiring. Then turning from Mary to John, the Savior addresses him, "Behold thy mother!" (John 19:27). John was a part of the trinity of Christ's inner circle—Peter, James, and John. He seemed to have been well loved by Christ, for he was called the disciple whom Jesus loved. Jesus entrusted John with the dearest earthly interest of Christ, the care of His widowed mother. John, who had leaned on the bosom of the Savior, was now given a closer place to His heart. The Scripture says, "And from that hour that disciple took her unto his own home" (v. 27).

CONCLUSION

Oh, my friend, in these sayings from the cross we see the light of God's love shining from heaven upon the entire world: "Greater love hath no man than this, that a man lay down his life for his friends" (15:13). Where could one see greater affection? Where could one detect such care? Where could one find love that is so high and lofty, but reaches so low as to pick up fallen man and to comfort troubled hearts? In these sayings from the cross we see the length, breadth, height, and depth of His love. This love is reaching to you. Even now, He reaches His hand of love to fallen humanity. Would you let this love draw you today and bring you out of the world into fellowship with Him? ✞

FACING OUR FEARS

"There is no fear in love; but perfect love casteth out fear: because fear hath torment. He that feareth is not made perfect in love" (1 John 4:18).

INTRODUCTION

The whole of the human race is beset by many and varied fears, which is a constant menace to happiness. Fear causes frustration and confusion, and much of the mental and physical sicknesses of our time are brought about through fear. But the Word of God says, "Fear hath torment" (1 John 4:18). Man is striving to be released and delivered from the tormenting fears of this complex age. Today in my message I am going to discuss with you some of the predominant fears that confront us in everyday life.

You need not be continually hounded by these fears, for the Word of God has an answer. Throughout the Word, God frequently says, "Fear not." God has made this appeal and given His commands to believers since the day He spoke to Abraham: "Fear not, Abram: I am thy shield, and thy exceeding great reward" (Gen. 15:1). From Abraham to John on the Isle of Patmos, the Word of God rings with these comforting words: "Fear not." What God commands He is able to perform. What God commands is paramount to a promise. God will not command you to do anything that He will not furnish grace for you to carry out.

Let us notice a few of the Bible characters to whom God said, "Fear not":

- Isaac—"Fear not, for I am with thee, and will bless thee" (Gen. 26:24).
- Jacob—"Fear not to go down into Egypt" (46:3).
- Daniel—"O man greatly beloved, fear not" (Dan. 10:19).

To all believers, God is saying, "Fear not, little flock; for it is your Father's good pleasure to give you the kingdom" (Luke 12:32).

There are different kinds of fears. Some people are afraid of the past, afraid of heredity, or afraid of failures of bygone days. Some are afraid of the call of God; they are afraid to yield themselves to God. Others are afraid of marriage. Some are afraid of sickness; others are afraid of old age. Some people have a fear of loneliness, a fear of man, a fear of a crowd, a fear of death, a fear of the loss of money, and even a fear of the future. But these fears are not God-given. The Scripture tells us, "For God hath not given us the spirit of fear; but of power, and of love, and of a sound mind" (2 Tim. 1:7). Fear is the result of sin.

We have the first biblical account of fear when the Lord God, walking in the cool of the day in the Garden of Eden, called for Adam and Eve. Adam said, "I heard thy voice in the garden, and I was afraid" (Gen. 3:10). Fear was the fruit of Adam's sin. From that day until this, mankind has been blighted by fear.

I. FEAR OF THE PAST

Now let us consider some of the common fears of our day. The first is the fear of the past. Some people seem to be unable to forget their unpleasant experiences and blunders of the past. Past mistakes, failures, and difficulties continually hamper their present and break down their self-confidence. This is the reason the apostle Paul said, "Forgetting those things which are behind, and reaching forth unto those things which are before" (Phil. 3:13). If there are victories, rejoice in them. If there were failures in the past, through Christ we can conquer them in the present.

Many people have the fear of heredity. They believe that their destiny has been shaped in the past. For example, I know a young man whose grandfather became an invalid because of arthritis, and every time that young man has an ache or pain in his joints the fear of crippling arthritis grips him. He feels certain that it runs in his family and he will be the next victim. It is always good to remember that heredity contributes only a part of what you are. As long as God controls your life, "all things work together for good to them that love God, to them who are the called according to his purpose" (Rom. 8:28). The Scripture promises, "As thy days, so shall thy strength be" (Deut. 33:25). For every fear that comes your way, you can find an answer in God's Word.

II. FEAR OF THE FUTURE

Then there is the fear of the future. Jesus said, "Men's hearts failing them for fear, and for looking after those things which are coming on the earth" (Luke 21:26). World affairs, tensions, pestilences, earthquakes, wars, rumors of war, famines, and missiles have only increased the anxiety concerning the future. Years ago, Sir Lloyd George said, "The future fills me with dread; I am afraid of what will happen." Once the Prince of Wales made this statement, "We have before us a sick world with fearful doubt." Another great statesman said, "At this moment, many hearts are failing them because of the difficulties which lie ahead." America's number one disease is heart disease, and men's hearts are failing them because of the fears of the future. What should be our attitude toward the future? Should the future affect a Christian in this manner? What should be our attitude? Jesus said:

- "And ye shall hear of wars and rumours of wars: see that ye be not troubled" (Matt. 24:6).

- "But when ye shall hear of wars and commotions, be not terrified" (Luke 21:9).
- "And when these things begin to come to pass, then look up, and lift up your heads; for your redemption draweth nigh" (v. 28).

The future holds hope for the believer; not despair. The foreground of the Christian is a bright prospect, for "the path of the just is as the shining light, that shineth more and more unto the perfect day" (Prov. 4:18). With every step into the future, the light of the Sun of Righteousness beams more brightly. As far as this world is concerned, I believe the future is dark. I believe that this civilization is headed for destruction. We are beset by many uncertainties and the whole world is a potential powder keg. The man who has fear of the future is prepared to live in this world only. I have made my plans for two worlds: the world that now is, and the world that is to come. In my soul are the seeds of immortality, and when this life comes to an end, there is a life beyond. I have experienced the power of an endless life, and regardless what happens to this present world—and we know it will happen—"he that doeth the will of God abideth for ever" (1 John 2:17). This gives us hope, "for now we see through a glass, darkly; but then face to face: now I know in part; but then shall I know even as also I am known" (1 Cor. 13:12).

The reason men lose their way through the desert and wilderness of this life is because they have lost the vision of the life to come and dropped to the level of mere brutes. If one has the vision of the life to come, it gives him courage to live in this present life. Much of the tension, fainting, and fear in today's world is because mankind has discarded his belief in the future life.

David said, "I had fainted, unless I had believed to see the goodness of the Lord in the land of the living" (Ps. 27:13). The apostle Paul asked, "What advantageth it me, if the dead rise not?" (1 Cor. 15:32). But Paul's hope in immortality and the resurrection—when the natural shall put on the spiritual, the earthly shall put on the heavenly, and the weak shall put on power—caused all his fears of the future to be dispelled and gave him courage to endure the burdens of the present. Paul saw things in their proper perspective, for he said, "For our light affliction, which is but for a moment, worketh for us a far more exceeding and eternal weight of glory" (2 Cor. 4:17).

Paul explained his philosophy of life by saying, "While we look not at the things which are seen, but at the things which are not seen: for the things which are seen are temporal; but the things which are not seen are eternal" (v. 18). Friend, if you look at things around about you—things that are temporal, things that are material, and things that are happening this day—your heart will faint. But Paul said, "We look not at the things which are seen, but at the things which are not seen" (v. 18). The things which are seen are temporal, but the things which are not seen are eternal. Paul pinned his hopes in the enduring things. He said, "For we know that if our earthly house of this tabernacle were dissolved, we have a building of God, an house not made with hands, eternal in the heavens" (5:1). A man who has this outlook need not fear death.

Death is an appointment that all men must meet: "And as it is appointed unto men once to die, but after this the judgment" (Heb. 9:27). Regardless of how many people die, man never seems to be quite prepared or ready to accept this. Associated with death are grief, agonies, pain, vacancies, and many other things that cast a shadow. But the Christian concept is different from that of the world. Death for a Christian is not a horrible ordeal. The apostle Paul said—and this should be our philosophy—"Whether we live therefore, or die, we are the Lord's" (Rom. 14:8). We belong to the Lord, and "for to me to live is Christ, and to die is gain" (Phil. 1:21).

To be absent from the body is to be present with the Lord. The psalmist said, "Precious in the sight of the Lord is the death of his saints" (116:15). John the Beloved said, "Blessed are the dead which die in the Lord from henceforth: Yea, saith the Spirit, that they may rest from their labours" (Rev. 14:13). "There remaineth therefore a rest to the people of God" (Heb. 4:9). All of these scriptures should banish the fear of death from the Christian's life. Jesus stands by your side today saying, "I am the resurrection, and the life: he that believeth in me, though he were dead, yet shall he live" (John 11:25). Hallelujah!

III. FEAR OF A LACK OF SECURITY

Another prominent fear is lack of security. It is an anxiety that has been common to every generation. It has caused sin to distort values; it has made men victims of worry and magnified the importance of materialism. God has given us a pattern of life that will dispel fear and worry:

> Which of you by taking thought can add one cubit unto his stature? And why take ye thought for raiment? Consider the lilies of the field, how they grow; they toil not, neither do they spin: and yet I say unto you, That even Solomon in all his glory was not arrayed like one of these. Wherefore, if God so clothe the grass of the field, which to day is, and to morrow is cast into the oven, shall he not much more clothe you, O ye of little faith? Therefore take no thought, saying, What shall we eat? or, What shall we drink? or, Wherewithal shall we be clothed? (For after all these things do the Gentiles seek:) for your heavenly Father knoweth that ye have need of all these things. But seek ye first the kingdom of God, and his righteousness; and all these things shall be added unto you (Matt. 6:27-33).

Hebrews 13:5 says, "Let your conversation be without covetousness; and be content with such things as ye have." The reason He admonishes us to be content with such things as we have is set forth in the following portion of the verse: "I will never leave thee, nor forsake thee."

Complete trust in God will dispel all fears of insecurity. Jesus promised, "Lo, I am with you alway, even unto the end of the world" (Matt. 28:20). The apostle Paul said, "But my God shall supply all your need according to his riches in glory by Christ Jesus" (Phil. 4:19).

D. L. Moody often quoted Isaiah 12:2: "I will trust, and not be afraid." And he often said you can travel first-class or second-class to heaven. First-class is, "I will trust, and not be afraid." Second-class is, "What time I'm afraid, I will trust."

My friend, if you are in financial strain, or if you feel insecure in your marriage, or if some other type of insecurity hounds you today, remember "whoso putteth his trust in the Lord shall be safe" (Prov. 29:25).

IV. FEAR OF MAN

Another common fear is the fear of man. The Book of Proverbs says, "The fear of man bringeth a snare" (29:25). The fear of man has kept many people from making a decision for the Lord Jesus Christ. They are afraid of the masses' criticism, or of the group's disapproval. Many have yielded to these social patterns, which has caused them to do many things against their conscience. They have allowed man to set their standards of right and wrong, instead of following God's absolute standard.

We must overcome the whims of the crowd and the persecution of the masses to determine our decision. Jesus said, "Fear not them which kill the body, but are not able to kill the soul: but rather fear him which is able to destroy both soul and body in hell" (Matt. 10:28). The Scripture tells us, "We may boldly say, The Lord is my helper, and I will not fear what man shall do unto me" (Heb. 13:6).

CONCLUSION

My friend, all of this hinges on a strong faith in Almighty God. Many of the fears that haunt you are the things that will never happen. They are mere phantoms, which do not exist. Your fears and worries are without ground and are useless. Nothing has ever been corrected through fear or worry. As the old hymn, "What a Friend We Have in Jesus," says:

O what peace we often forfeit,
O what needless pain we bear,
All because we do not carry
Everything to God in prayer.

Bring your worries and anxieties to Jesus. He alone is the answer for the cares and concerns of your life. Don't forfeit the peace that is found in Jesus. Don't continue to bear needless pain. Carry everything to God in prayer now. ✞

GOD'S LOVE FOR THE BACKSLIDER

"Return, ye backsliding children, and I will heal your backslidings" (Jer. 3:22).

INTRODUCTION

The study of the history of the human race will reveal God's love for the backslider. Since the day that Adam and Eve fell in the Garden of Eden, man has strayed and wandered from God. But God in His infinite love and tender mercy has always called him back. Man has tried the patience of God with his perpetual backsliding and wanderings. Yet, God has not wavered in His love and His care for those who have strayed from His side. He has always been constant in His concern and compassion. When Judah persisted in backsliding, He showed His concern by asking the question, "Why then is this people of Jerusalem slidden back by a perpetual backsliding?" (Jer. 8:5).

A perpetual backsliding is a continual backsliding or a continued wandering and straying from Almighty God. Israel had backslidden so many times until God had said to the prophet Hosea, "And my people are bent to backsliding from me" (Hos. 11:7). Notice the phrase "bent to backsliding." How appropriate for these times. Of Israel, again, Hosea said, "For Israel slideth back as a backsliding heifer" (4:16). Yet, these backslidings did not exhaust the unsearchable treasures of God's love. He cried out, "I am weary with repenting" (Jer. 15:6). Yet, when they did repent God heard their cries and restored them to their former state. He said, "I am pressed under you, as a cart is pressed that is full of sheaves" (Amos 2:13). He still remembered them when they were willing to return to Him.

Like many other eras of human history, this age seems to be an age of backsliding, and there is nothing more damaging to the cause of Christ and that has brought more reproach on the cause of Christ than the backsliding of professors. The purpose of this message is not to condone the backsliding or to license it. Neither do I mean to infer that men cannot live without committing sin or practicing sin. My purpose is to show you that though you have strayed from God and have wandered from His bleeding side, still He reaches out to you and looks upon you with eyes of love, ready to embrace you again in His everlasting arms.

I. BACKSLIDING IS A CREEPING PARALYSIS

Very few people who backslide actually want to go back on God. Backsliding comes upon them like creeping paralysis and has them in its clutches before they are aware of it. It enters their lives like a microscopic germ and they are not aware of it until it has eaten away the vitals of their experience. Backsliding is not a crisis, but a process. No one falls into open sin suddenly after he has known Christ. Backsliding comes by degrees, and it is dangerous to backslide to any degree because the sinner cannot regulate sin. With sin at the helm he becomes a slave and a servant, and we never know how far sin will lead us. At this point it would be good for every Christian to examine himself to see if he has backslidden in any manner.

When a Christian fails to pray, to read his Bible, to give the portion that belongs to God, to attend God's house, or to fulfill any of the commands of Scripture, he is backsliding.

My friend, you can weaken yourself through spiritual neglect until the time will come when you can no longer resist the temptations of Satan. The Christian's life is one of spiritual resistance. The Bible says, "Resist the devil, and he will flee from you" (James 4:7). But when you have failed to carry out God's commands, your spiritual resistance is weakened and you have no power to overcome, therefore, you fall. If you will acknowledge your backslidings and confess them, you can correct the error of your ways. Otherwise, your backslidings will reprove you. If you have looked into your own heart and have detected misgivings there, why not cry out with the psalmist, "Hold up my goings in thy paths, that my footsteps slip not. I have called upon thee, for thou wilt hear me, O God: incline thine ear unto me, and hear my speech. Shew thy marvelous lovingkindness, O thou that savest by thy right hand them which put their trust in thee from those that rise up against them. Keep me as the apple of the eye, hide me under the shadow of thy wings" (17:5-8).

II. GOD CALLS THE BACKSLIDER TO RETURN TO HIM

No individual or group has ever gone back on God but that He calls them back or beckons them to return. Regardless of how far away they have strayed or how vile their lives, God calls them back. Some people feel they have gone too far and there is no chance or opportunity for them to return. But regardless of how deep your sins, or criminal your actions, the Father is saying, "Return, ye backsliding children, and I will heal your backslidings" (Jer. 3:22). The Bible says Israel sinned: "Thou hast spoken and done evil things as thou couldest" (v. 5). In other words, there was no restraint to her sinfulness. Yet verse 7 says, "And I said after she had done all these things, Turn thou unto me." Israel had dealt treacherously with God, and Jeremiah puts it like this: "Surely as a wife treacherously departeth from her husband, so have ye dealt treacherously with me, O house of Israel, saith the Lord" (v. 20). God could have put her away and given her a bill of divorcement, but instead He says, "Return and I will heal your backslidings." When Judah had backslidden, Isaiah called the heavens to record against him: "Hear, O heavens, and give ear, O earth: for the Lord hath spoken, I have nourished and brought up children, and they have rebelled against me. . . . They have forsaken the Lord, they have provoked the Holy One of Israel unto anger, they are gone away backward" (1:2, 4).

Listen to this call of love. It was to this people—the people who had gone away backward, a people who had forsaken the Lord, a people who had rebelled against Him. God said, "Come now, and let us reason together, saith the Lord: though your sins be as scarlet, they shall be as white as snow; though they be red like crimson, they shall be as wool" (v. 18). He was calling upon a people who had rebelled against Him, who had sinned against Him in the face of His mercy and love, to come and reason with Him.

Oh, the great God of heaven condescends to men of low estate and God our Maker comes down to reason with those whom He created, offering them restoration. What love! What mercy!

Another Bible example of God's willingness to accept backsliders is seen in His dealings with Ephraim. The testimony against Ephraim was thus:

- "O Ephraim, what shall I do unto thee? O Judah, what shall I do unto thee? for your goodness is as morning cloud, and as the early dew it goeth away" (Hos. 6:4).
- "Ephraim, he hath mixed himself among the people; Ephraim is a cake not turned" (7:8).
- "Ephraim also is like a silly dove without heart" (v. 11).
- "They return, but not to the most High: they are like a deceitful bow" (v. 16).

- "As for Ephraim, their glory shall fly away like a bird" (9:11).
- "Their heart is divided" (10:2).
- "Therefore they shall be as the morning cloud, and as the early dew that passeth away, as the chaff that is driven with the whirlwind out of the floor, and as the smoke out of the chimney" (13:3).

All of these scriptures show the instability and faithlessness of Ephraim. But in spite of all of the waywardness, I hear God asking, "How shall I give thee up, Ephraim? how shall I deliver thee, Israel? how shall I make thee as Admah? how shall I set thee as Zeboim? mine heart is turned within me, my repentings are kindled together" (11:8). Then I hear Him say again, "I drew them with cords of a man, with bands of love" (v. 4).

III. GOD WILL HEAL YOUR BACKSLIDING

Backsliders, hear the words of Hosea: "Come, and let us return unto the Lord: for he hath torn, and he will heal us; he hath smitten, and he will bind us up" (6:1).

Man has been known to drive a wayward son from his home, but God says to wayward souls, "I will heal their backsliding, I will love them freely" (14:4). In Psalm 89:30-32, God says, "If his children forsake my law, and walk not in my judgments; if they break my statutes, and keep not my commandments; then will I visit their transgression with the rod, and their iniquity with stripes." Now listen to this: "Nevertheless my lovingkindness will I not utterly take from him, nor suffer my faithfulness to fail" (v. 33). This shows God's unfailing love for the man who has failed Him and has gone back on Him.

The parable of the prodigal son, which is called the pearl of all parables, is certainly a portrait of God's pardoning love for the backslider. This story reveals the willingness of God for every prodigal to return, and not only the willingness but the compassion and love toward those who return. When the boy decided to return home, the memory of his father's character and never varying love assured him of acceptance. If you are a backslider, remember that the Lord not only requests you to return, but patiently awaits your return. "But God commendeth his love toward us, in that, while we were yet sinners, Christ died for us" (Rom. 5:8). Love never fails and love never deserts us. Jesus said, "Him that cometh to me I will in no wise cast out" (John 6:37).

Not only does He await your return, but He is seeking your return. The love of God is broader than the measure of man's mind, and the heart of the Eternal is most wonderfully kind. Now here is the picture of true love. One day as the father looked out across the field, he saw his son returning dirty, tattered, and unkempt. What a repulsive tramp he was! But his father had compassion on him. He ran to meet him; he fell on his neck and kissed him. He did not say to his son that after a time of probation, or after he had paid some penalty for the evil he had done, or gone through some purifying process, that he would accept him. But immediately he took him into the fold. But this love did not stop here. His father said to the servants, "Bring forth the best robe, and put it on him; and put a ring on his hand, and shoes on his feet: And bring hither the fatted calf, and kill it; and let us eat, and be merry: For this my son was dead, and is alive again; he was lost, and is found" (Luke 15:22-24).

CONCLUSION

If you are backslidden, God's love is offering you the best. He is saying, "Bring forth the best robe, and put it on him." Backslider, why not win your way back to God today? Allow the goodness of God to lead you to repentance.

Remember your backsliding began in forsaking prayer, and your healing will begin with renewed prayer. God is "not willing that any should perish, but that all should come to repentance" (2 Peter 3:9). God's Word says, "Remember therefore from whence thou art fallen, and repent, and do the first works" (Rev. 2:5). Remember the time when you first accepted Jesus as your Savior and Healer and the joyous experience you had. Remember the refreshing moments of prayer and the daily blessings upon your life. Remember, and return. "Return, ye backsliding children, and I will heal your backslidings" (Jer. 3:22). ✞

HOLINESS—GOD'S STANDARD FOR LIVING

"But as he which hath called you is holy, so be ye holy in all manner of conversation; because it is written, Be ye holy; for I am holy" (1 Peter 1:15-16).

INTRODUCTION

Holiness is God's standard of living for His people. Among theologians and Christians there is much debate and controversy concerning the subject of holiness. Therefore, it is necessary for us to search out a biblical definition. Holiness is the true way of life. It is not some indescribable rapture of glory that can be obtained by only a few of God's elite. It is not merely a rapturous triumph somewhere in the vague height but a life lived in conformity to Jesus Christ.

Holiness is not an exceptional privilege to which an inner circle of God's favorites are admitted. But it is the rule and design for life, for all the followers of the Lord who will make the surrender. Holiness is the highway to the Father's house. It is our inheritance. Holiness is the life of sacrifice, self-denial, separation, and surrender. It is not something within you, nor is it a state of being that is reached by personal goodness or abstinence. Holiness does not rest in human measurements, but in Christ.

I. HOLINESS IS CHRISTLIKE

Some people bind heavy burdens that are unbiblical upon men and impose their prejudices and label them as holiness. But the biblical standard is strict enough. In search for heart purity we need not be those who set unreachable goals, but all our convictions must rest upon the Word of God. This is the only standard God requires. Anything beneath God's standard is of the world, and any extreme beyond God's standard is pharisaical. Jesus Christ is the embodiment of holiness. The Bible says, "But of him are ye in Christ Jesus, who of God is made unto us wisdom, and righteousness, and sanctification, and redemption" (1 Cor. 1:30). Therefore, holiness is Christlike. It is a reflection of Christ in our lives; it is a reproduction of Christ's life in our attitude and actions. This was the kind of living that made the Christians of the early church effective. Christ, the embodiment of holiness, was seen in the lives of His professed followers: "And they took knowledge of them, that they had been with Jesus" (Acts 4:13).

Many people think of holiness as a doctrine to be discussed and not a life to be lived. Therefore, they become occupied with the doctrine and not with the practice. The doctrine lived is much more forceful than the doctrine proclaimed. The Word of God says, "Ye are our epistle written in our hearts, known and read of all men: Forasmuch as ye are manifestly declared to be the epistle of Christ ministered by us, written not with ink, but with the Spirit of the living God; not in tables of stone, but in fleshly tables of the heart. And such trust have we through Christ to God-ward" (2 Cor. 3:2-4).

The name *Christian* has come to mean anyone who adheres to the faith, whether traditionally or experientially. But in the early church the people were first called Christians because they were devoted followers of the Lord Jesus Christ, and people could see in them a reflection of the Son of God. The apostle John wrote:

- "He that saith he abideth in him ought himself also so to walk, even as he walked" (1 John 2:6).

- "And every man that hath this hope in him purifieth himself, even as he is pure" (3:3).
- "Because as he is, so are we in the world" (4:17).

God commands us to live a life of holiness. He is saying for us to be like Christ in thought, word, and deed—to know Him in the daily experience of life and let the beauty of Christ be seen in our lives. There is no need to make holiness a vague mystical doctrine, hard to be understood, and almost impossible to obtain, for holiness is a requirement of the Lord. God does not require anything of man except He gives grace to carry it out.

II. HOLINESS IS A COMMAND OF GOD

God has commanded us to be holy. The Bible says, "But as he which hath called you is holy, so be ye holy in all manner of conversation; because it is written, Be ye holy; for I am holy" (1 Peter 1:15-16). A holy God wants a holy people. Three times in the Book of Deuteronomy, the Bible says, "Thou art an holy people unto the Lord thy God" (7:6; 14:2, 21). All of God's possessions must be holy. While it is true that God has commanded us to be holy, we must always remember that whatever God has commanded, He is able to perform. All of God's commands are essentially promises.

The Scripture says, "Be ye holy; for I am holy" (1 Peter 1:16). At least four times in the Book of Leviticus, this command is given to all the people of Israel (11:45; 19:2; 20:7, 26). Our calling to be children of God is a holy calling and has imposed an obligation upon us. Let us then consider the holiness of Him who has called us.

Israel sang the song of Moses when they had crossed the Red Sea. A portion of that song declares the holiness of God: "Who is like unto thee, O Lord, among the gods? who is like thee, glorious in holiness" (Ex. 15:11). Even the seraphim in glory cry, "Holy, holy, holy, is the Lord of hosts" (Isa. 6:3). His throne is called "the throne of his holiness" (Ps. 47:8). Divine sovereignty is always connected with holiness. He has a throne of holiness for which He is to be feared by all men. He has a throne of grace for which all those who are redeemed love Him. He has a throne of glory that inhabits the praises of all His creation. All His decrees, acts, and commands are holy, for His name is holy. He has spoken in His holiness. He has sworn by His holiness. He is the Holy One, the High and Lofty One who inhabits eternity. And He said, "For I am the Lord your God: ye shall therefore sanctify yourselves, and ye shall be holy; for I am holy" (Lev. 11:44).

He has made it possible "that we might be partakers of His holiness" (Heb. 12:10). Since holiness is the very nature of God, we then become partakers of His divine nature—"According as his divine power hath given unto us all things that pertain unto life and godliness, through the knowledge of him that hath called us to glory and virtue: whereby are given unto us exceeding great and precious promises: that by these ye might be partakers of the divine nature, having escaped the corruption that is in the world through lust" (2 Peter 1:3-4). The Bible says, "According as he hath chosen us in him before the foundation of the world, that we should be holy and without blame before him in love" (Eph. 1:4). The unholiness of these times calls for pulpits to become more vocal on the subject. I am aware that there is sensitiveness about the subject of holiness that causes ministers to shy away from it. Most people resent holiness because it is condemnation of their own sins. Holiness deals with the sin question in men's lives and if Christians are to make it through to heaven, they must quit straining at practical holiness. Holiness is not an experience that happens at death. There are those who only make saints out of the dead. But the Scripture requires sanctity in living. In Romans 12:1, Paul sets forth sanctity and holiness in living: "I beseech you therefore, brethren, by the mercies of God, that ye present your bodies a living sacrifice, holy, acceptable unto God, which is your reasonable service."

III. GOD COMMANDS HOLINESS OF BEHAVIOR

God requires that we be holy in our behavior. The apostle Paul said, "Ye are witnesses, and God also, how holily and justly and unblameably we behaved ourselves among you that believe" (1 Thess. 2:10). He declared to those around him that he had lived a life of holiness in their midst. In writing to the aged women, Paul admonished them "that they be in behaviour as becometh holiness" (Titus 2:3), or more literally, that they should show themselves as becometh holiness. The Greek word rendered "in behaviour," includes dress, appearance, conversation, and manner. It includes an outward deportment dependent upon something more internal. No end of harm is done to the cause of Christ by the unholy and inconsistent living of those who are called by the name of the Lord. God requires that Christians be examples in conduct. One who professes true holiness will strive to adorn his experience and make it lovely and beautiful in the eyes of those around about him. He will hate backbiting, cheating, dishonesty, unfair dealings, and will pay his just and honest debts. There needs to be a higher standard of personal holiness in the circles of Christianity today.

There must be a distinguishing tone that marks a difference between the saints of God and the world. The standards of the world are diametrically opposed to the standards of holiness. God declared in Psalm 97:10, "Ye that love the Lord, hate evil." The psalmist declared, "Therefore I esteem all thy precepts concerning all things to be right; and I hate every false way" (119:128). Holiness in a man's heart causes him to hate what God hates and to love what God loves.

While the worldling tries to conform to this world, the holy man strives to be conformed to the image of the Son of God. The holy man has set his affections on things above and not on things of the earth. We must not allow the standards of the world to shape our opinions, ideals, or decisions. The world is a sworn and relentless foe to the high life of holiness, and any compromise with it will distract your attention from the Holy One of God. Holiness is a separated life, but not an isolated life.

IV. HOLINESS IS A SEPARATED LIFE

According to the Scripture, one can live blameless and without rebuke in the midst of a crooked and perverse nation. This is an insulated life. This can best be explained by this illustration: The electric wires bringing current into your home are insulated, which means that they are separated from the earth by a nonconductor. Therefore, the holiness of God insulates us as Christians and separates us for the service of God. The Red Sea became the separation line between the Egyptians and Israelites. We never read of the Israelites singing while in Egypt, but when they had crossed the Red Sea and left Egypt behind, they became joyous and sang the song of Moses while the maidens beat the timbrels and danced the dance of victory.

If a Christian is to be happy and joyful, he must become all out for Jesus Christ and be separated from the world. Holiness will cause a man to abstain from some things. Abstinence within itself is not holiness; it is the fruit of holiness. A man is not holy simply because he does not do certain things, but he doesn't do certain things because he is holy. Holiness is of the heart and the outward external life is but the fruit of holiness. Putting off or laying aside certain things has never made men holy. This the Pharisees had always done, but Jesus Christ called them "whited sepulchres, which indeed appear beautiful outward, but are within full of dead men's bones" (Matt. 23:27).

While it is true that one cannot make himself holy through the absence of certain things, it is also true that the Bible says, "That ye put off concerning the former conversation the old man, which is corrupt according to the deceitful lusts; and be renewed in the spirit of your mind; and that ye put on the new man, which after God is created in righteousness and true holiness" (Eph. 4:22-24). In the verses following these scriptures, a life of holiness is outlined. Notice what Paul says: "Wherefore putting away lying. . . . Be ye angry, and sin not. . . . Neither give place to the devil. Let him that stole steal no more. . . . Let no corrupt communication proceed out of your mouth. . . . And grieve not the holy Spirit of God. . . . Let all bitterness, and wrath, and anger, and clamour, and evil speaking, be put away from you. . . . And be ye kind one to another, tenderhearted, forgiving one another, even as God for Christ's sake hath forgiven you" (vv. 25-32). This is practical holiness.

No doubt some of you are laboring within yourself in laying aside the world. You have read scriptures like these:

- "Lay aside every weight, and the sin which doth so easily beset us" (Heb. 12:1).
- "Dearly beloved, let us cleanse ourselves from all filthiness of the flesh and spirit, perfecting holiness in the fear of God" (2 Cor. 7:1).
- "And they that are Christ's have crucified the flesh with the affections and lusts" (Gal. 5:24).
- "But I keep under my body, and bring it into subjection: lest that by any means, when I have preached to others, I myself should be a castaway" (1 Cor. 9:27).
- "Mortify therefore your members which are upon the earth" (Col. 3:5).

But you say, "How can I do this?" This is not done through an effort of your own; it is only done as we yield ourselves to God. Here is where so many people err: after they have struggled in the flesh and have failed, and are disappointed time after time, they give up in despair. But we lay aside every sin that besets us, we cleanse ourselves, we crucify ourselves, mortify the flesh, and keep our bodies under subjection by yielding to the Lord Jesus Christ. Then, He does the work in us.

The Bible says, "Even so now yield your members servants to righteousness unto holiness" (Rom. 6:19). Holiness is both subjective and objective. We must first submit ourselves to God, and then God can do the work in us. Oh, my Christian friend, as you yield yourself to God, your holiness shall be perfected, you will grow in grace, and you will abound in love. Mercy, grace, and peace will be multiplied and one grace after another will be added to your life. Continually walking with Him brings us to "the measure of the stature of the fulness of Christ" (Eph. 4:13) that we "may grow up into him in all things" (v. 15).

Those who would frown at the thought of holiness, and for those whom the doctrine of holiness repels, listen to Hebrews 12:14: "Follow peace with all men, and holiness, without which no man shall see the Lord." This is a positive but sobering thought. The Bible says, "Blessed are the pure in heart: for they shall see God" (Matt. 5:8). Revelation 20:6 says, "Blessed and holy is he that hath part in the first resurrection." Our inheritance in heaven is said to be incorruptible and undefiled. Heaven is a holy place—a holy city inhabited by holy creatures—for everything in heaven is holy. The creatures in glory rest not day or night, saying, "Holy, holy, holy, is the Lord of hosts" (Isa. 6:3). The song that is sung in praise to the Lamb is a praise of holiness. They worship the Holy God in the beauty of holiness.

CONCLUSION

My friend, if you are planning to go to heaven you must become accustomed to holiness in the here and now, for heaven is a place of holiness: "And there shall in no wise enter into it any thing that defileth, neither whatsoever worketh abomination, or maketh a lie" (Rev. 21:27). In the light of this, the apostle Peter tells us what manner of people we ought to be:

> But the day of the Lord will come as a thief in the night; in the which the heavens shall pass away with a great noise, and the elements shall melt with fervent heat, the earth also and the works that are therein shall be burned up. Seeing then that all these things shall be dissolved, what manner of persons ought ye to be in all holy conversation and godliness, looking for and hasting unto the coming of the day of God, wherein the heavens being on fire shall be dissolved, and the elements shall melt with fervent heat? Nevertheless we, according to his promise, look for new heavens and a new earth, wherein dwelleth righteousness. Wherefore, beloved, seeing that ye look for such things, be diligent that ye may be found of him in peace, without spot, and blameless (2 Peter 3:10-14).

Please bow your head with me in prayer. ✞

HOPE THOU IN GOD

"As the hart panteth after the water brooks, so panteth my soul after thee, O God. My soul thirsteth for God, for the living God: when shall I come and appear before God? My tears have been my meat day and night, while they continually say unto me, Where is thy God? When I remember these things, I pour out my soul in me: for I had gone with the multitude, I went with them to the house of God, with the voice of joy and praise, with a multitude that kept holyday. Why art thou cast down, O my soul? and why art thou disquieted in me? hope thou in God: for I shall yet praise him for the help of his countenance" (Ps. 42:1-5).

INTRODUCTION

Here is a picture of a man talking to his soul. The question is raised as to why a disturbance existed in his soul. Direction is then given as to what his soul should do, followed with the assurance that he shall soon have the help his soul needs.

This admonition was given at one of the most difficult times in life. Most Bible scholars attribute this song to David and center the time of the song when David was a fugitive from his own kingdom. You will recall that during David's life Absalom, his son, usurped the kingdom and David was forced to flee for his life. He was pursued by his own son. The object of this pursuit was to overthrow and, if necessary, kill David in order that the kingdom might be secured for Absalom.

One could almost place himself in David's shoes and feel something of the load and the oppression. His soul was torn between allegiance to his kingdom and love toward his son. He became discouraged beyond words. David's own words tell us of his discouragement: "My tears have been my meat day and night, while they continually say unto me, Where is thy God?" (Ps. 42:3). "O my God, my soul is cast down within me: therefore will I remember thee from the land of Jordan, and of the Hermonites, from the hill Mizar" (v. 6).

I. DAVID LONGED FOR BETTER DAYS

The discouragement that David experienced at this time no doubt arose from the fact that somehow he had failed in the rearing of Absalom. Now his own son was willing to betray him and perhaps even kill him. The loyal love that he felt for his son deterred him from taking military action and saving the kingdom. Yet, his loyalty to his people forced him at least to make a show in an effort to regain the throne that he had to leave so abruptly. Facing these conditions, it is no wonder his tears were his meat day and night. This admonition to his soul to hope in God was giving the cause of his homesickness for better days: "When I remember these things, I pour out my soul in me: for I had gone with the multitude, I went with them to the house of God, with the voice of joy and praise, with a multitude that kept holyday" (Ps. 42:4).

Now in the wilderness fleeing for his own life, he could remember those better days of his life when the adulation of the crowd was a part of his living, when in the house of God he lifted his voice in joy and praise. Now these days were gone and he longed for a return of those days. Consequently, he admonished his soul to hope in God. If it were not enough that his son would thus betray him, trouble on top of trouble seems to be his portion: "Deep calleth unto deep at the noise of thy waterspouts: all thy waves and thy billows are gone over me" (v. 7). The old saying "When it rains, it pours" seems to be true in David's case.

David likened his difficulties to waterspouts and to waves that continually overwhelmed him. When he would get up, another wave would crash into his chest sending him down so that trouble heaped on trouble seemed to be his portion. David did not depend on his own resources at this time.

II. DAVID MADE GOD THE OBJECT OF HIS TRUST

"For I will not trust in my bow, neither shall my sword save me" (Ps. 44:6). David made God the great object of his trust at this time. Human instrumentality and human means were at his disposal, yet he placed his confidence in God. The armies that had followed him were loyal to the utmost degree; they were ready and willing to fight for David until the last drop of blood had been shed. Yet David in this hour of extremity did not call upon his armies to help him; he told his soul to hope in God.

David did not depend on the wealth that was available to him at this time to help him out of the difficulties in which he found himself involved. He recognized the fact that riches were of little value when a man's soul was tormented and torn within him and needed uplifting. Nor did David depend on the loyalty of his subjects to give him the hope that was needed at this time. His whole trust and hope was in the Lord of Glory: "Through thee will we push down our enemies: through thy name will we tread them under that rise up against us" (v. 5).

The dignity of man when he finds himself in trouble is to see if he cannot do something about the condition. David, however, recognized the utter futility of attempting to raise himself out of his difficulties by his own bootstraps. He rejected all human resources and said to his soul, "Hope thou in God" (42:5). David's confidence was in the Lord. The following verses graphically tell us of his confidence in the Lord God Almighty to give him the help that he needed: "For I shall yet praise him for the help of his countenance" (v. 5); "Yet the Lord will command his lovingkindness in the daytime, and in the night his song shall be with me, and my prayer unto the God of my life" (v. 8). What tremendous confidence David was exhibiting in God! He expressed the confidence that God's lovingkindness would be his light in the daytime and songs in the night would be his portion.

Despite oppression of the enemies, David said, "Why go I mourning because of the oppression of the enemy? As with a sword in my bones, mine enemies reproach me; while they say daily unto me, Where is thy God? Why art thou cast down, O my soul? and why art thou disquieted within me? hope thou in God: for I shall yet praise him, who is the health of my countenance, and my God" (vv. 9-11).

III. HOPE THOU IN GOD

Your days, like David's, may be dark; you may not see much hope for the future. You have the same recourse for help as did David in his day. Trials may beset you on every hand and the ways seem dark and foreboding, yet I feel you should take the same confidence in God as did David. "Hope thou in God." You may be fighting a battle against the spiraling costs of living; you may be beset on every hand with pressures of all sorts. It may be a burden and a trial to make one payday stretch into the next. You may hardly see where the future holds much in the way of economics for you, yet I would say, "Hope thou in God."

There may be wars and strife in the world on every hand. Yet your hope is in God and you should tell your soul, "Hope thou in God." Exercise as did David your hope in God: "As for me, I will call upon God; and the Lord shall save me" (Ps. 55:16). I may be talking to some of you who are outside of Christ, who daily have troubles in your life. Sin has made you despair of hope and you feel that there is no help for you at all. I would say to you, as did David, "Hope thou in God."

Upon another occasion, the psalmist David said, "From the end of the earth will I cry unto thee, when my heart is overwhelmed: lead me to the rock that is higher than I" (61:2). Is sin making life miserable for you? Have you gotten to the place where nothing satisfies? Then I would say to you, "Hope thou in God." The psalmist had such an experience when he said, "The sorrows of death compassed me, and the pains of hell gat hold upon me: I found trouble and sorrow. Then called I upon the name of the Lord; O Lord, I beseech thee, deliver my soul. Gracious is the Lord, and righteous; yea, our God is merciful" (116:3-5).

In that same psalm, David said, "For thou hast delivered my soul from death, mine eyes from tears, and my feet from falling" (v. 8). And in Psalm 55:18 he declared, "He hath delivered my soul in peace." My friend, hope in God, for He will deliver you and He will give you peace in your heart in the time of storm. Some of you may feel yourselves beyond the help of the Lord and you may feel there is no hope for you. If you find yourself in such a condition, I would say, "Hope thou in God."

Job, in the midst of his desolation, sickness, horror, and anguish of soul, while reaching for hope and help, cried out, "But he knoweth the way that I take: when he hath tried me, I shall come forth as gold" (23:10). My friend, God is near you now to help you in your time of need. Hope thou in God and you shall yet praise Him who is your help and your strength. I may be speaking to some of you who feel that you cannot go any further and that you must have relief, that you can scarcely put one foot in front of another and you do not see how you can go on any longer. I think David experienced such a feeling. He cried out, "My soul thirsteth for God, for the living God: when shall I come and appear before God?" (Ps. 42:2).

CONCLUSION

That longing for soul satisfaction will soon be yours; the Lord will not tarry forever. You'll not always be thirsty; you'll not always go on in your despair. "Hope thou in God." In the midst of your desolation and in the midst of your trial, Christ extends to you the hope of His soon coming. I would suggest to you that God will satisfy that soul-thirsting for the Lord of Glory.

Hold on a little longer, my friend. Hope thou in God and we shall yet praise Him in joyfulness and in glory in days to come. If I am speaking to those who are at one of the most difficult periods in their lives, then I would say to you, "Hope thou in God." If you feel that there is no hope at all and that you have summoned up all of your own resources and you have tried your best to seek a way out of all this mess, I would ask you today, my friend, to cast away your own confidence and hope in God. Lean not on your own understanding, but trust Him completely and entirely and He will lead you out. If your days are dark and you do not see much hope in the future, I would suggest again to you that all your hope should be in God. If sin has been the trouble in your life and you see no way out of it at all, remember that God is faithful and He will answer your cry and will deliver your soul if you will call upon Him today. To those who are discouraged and feel that it is useless to press on, remember our Lord is coming soon. "Why art thou cast down, O my soul? Hope thou in God."

Will you cast yourself upon the mercies of the Lord and trust Him completely today and for all eternity? Will you consider your ways and look to God today? Whatever your problem, whatever your perplexities, whatever your despair, hope in God and He'll take you through. Let us pray. ✞

RUNNING FROM GOD

"Now the word of the Lord came unto Jonah the son of Amittai, saying, Arise, go to Nineveh, that great city, and cry against it; for their wickedness is come up before me. But Jonah rose up to flee unto Tarshish from the presence of the Lord, and went down to Joppa; and he found a ship going to Tarshish: so he paid the fare thereof, and went down into it, to go with them unto Tarshish from the presence of the Lord" (Jonah 1:1-3).

INTRODUCTION

The story of Jonah and the whale has been a subject of much controversy. It has been considered by some as merely a myth. But Jesus Christ authenticated the story when He said, "There shall no sign be given to it, but the sign of the prophet Jonas: for as Jonas was three days and three nights in the whale's belly; so shall the Son of man be three days and three nights in the heart of the earth" (Matt. 12:39-40).

God called Jonah to go to Nineveh, the great metropolis of the Assyrian monarchy. Nineveh was an imminent city of that day, a city of over one-half million people, and one of extreme wickedness. Nahum called it "the bloody city . . . full of lies and robbery" (3:1). Jonah was called upon to go and cry against this city, but to avoid the will of God, Jonah rose up to flee from the presence of the Lord. God had called upon him to go east, but he turned his face toward the west and went down to the port of Joppa and found a ship going to Tarsus. Jonah took the first ship leaving port. He was not bound for any place in particular, but desired to get away from the presence of the Lord. When Jonah failed to go to Nineveh as God had directed, he lost his sense of direction.

Anyone who fails to obey the commands of God, or to take orders from the Lord, loses his direction in life. The Bible says, "It is not in man that walketh to direct his steps" (Jer. 10:23). The journey from Joppa to Tarsus on the coast of Spain was far more hazardous than the journey that God had called him to make. Those who avoid the will of God think themselves to take an easier route. There is no dissatisfaction like the dissatisfaction of being out of the will of God. There is no burden harder to be borne than the burden of going against God. Many people fail to carry out the will of God because they feel it is hard and exacting. They are like those who followed the Lord for the loaves and fishes. When called upon to make a decision they said, "This is an hard saying; who can hear it?" (John 6:60). Or they are like the man who was given one talent, which he wrapped in a napkin and buried, saying, "I knew thee that thou art an hard man, reaping where thou hast not sown, and gathering where thou hast not strawed" (Matt. 25:24).

It is true that Christianity is a cross and it is a yoke, but Christ said, "My yoke is easy, and my burden is light" (11:30). The way outside of the will of God is always hazardous. The wise man Solomon said, "The way of transgressors is hard" (Prov. 13:15).

Jonah ran into one difficulty after another when he ran from God. The ship had no sooner put to sea until the elements began to fight against him. Some people wonder why they have so many difficulties; it is simply because they are going in the wrong direction. This is the reason the Lord said, "Turn ye, turn ye from your evil ways; for why will ye die, O house of Israel?" (Ezek. 33:11).

I. GOD WILL PURSUE YOU

The Bible says the Lord sent out a great wind into the sea and there was a mighty tempest. The Lord God pursued Jonah with a mighty wind. The Word of God tells us, "He bringeth the wind out of his treasuries" (Ps. 135:7). The wind became a messenger of wrath to warn a wayward man. The Scripture says, "Even the wind and the sea obey him" (Mark 4:41). Solomon said, "Who hath gathered the wind in his fists? who hath bound the waters in a garment?" (Prov. 30:4). In the words of the psalmist, God sends forth the stormy winds, fulfilling His word. Down in the sides of the little ship on the Mediterranean Sea, the wind located Jonah. The winds howled in weird tones, the sea opened its mouth, and lightning blazed across the heavens. The rolling thunder vibrated the little ship, while the raging winds snapped and cracked the canvas of the sails, the ropes beat against the mast, and the rigging of the ship rattled. God's judgment reached forth its arms for a runaway prophet.

The Scripture says, "There was a mighty tempest in the sea" (Jonah 1:4). Whenever one runs from God, he always runs into a tempest, for the Bible says, "The wicked are like the troubled sea, when it cannot rest, whose waters cast up mire and dirt. There is no peace, saith my God, to the wicked" (Isa. 57:20-21). But when Jesus enters the picture, He says to the raging storm, "Peace, be still" (Mark 4:39). "Thou rulest the raging of the sea: when the waves thereof arise, thou stillest them" (Ps. 89:9). "He maketh the storm a calm, so that the waves thereof are still" (107:29).

Jonah soon learned that the words of the psalmist were true: "Who layeth the beams of his chambers in the waters: who maketh the clouds his chariot: who walketh upon the wings of the wind" (104:3). He was made aware that God controlled the sea and shut up the sea with doors when it breaks forth, and measured the waters in the hollow of His hands.

There is a tempest in every human breast when one endeavors to flee from the presence of the Lord. Much of the frustration, confusion, and mental disturbances of our day, are brought about by the lack of willingness on the part of humanity to conform to the will and to the call of Almighty God. Some are fleeing from the presence of the Lord to avoid a call of God, or a service for God. Others are endeavoring to evade circumstances, while others wish to hide their sins. If you are running from a call of God, remember God does not require anything of you but what He will give you grace to carry out, for He has said, "My grace is sufficient for thee" (2 Cor. 12:9).

II. YOU CANNOT ESCAPE THE PRESENCE OF GOD

If you are running from God trying to evade circumstances, remember the only way you will ever overcome the circumstances that you encounter is to face them through the power of the Holy Spirit. If you are trying to flee from your sins, or find a hiding place for your iniquity, there is only one safe place for you, and that is beneath the ruby red beads of blood that flowed from the crimson Calvary.

The Bible declares: "Thou hast set our iniquities before thee, our secret sins in the light of thy countenance" (Ps. 90:8); "The heavens shall reveal his iniquity; and the earth shall rise up against him" (Job 20:27); "For there is nothing covered, that shall not be revealed; neither hid, that shall not be known" (Luke 12:2). Our hearts are before the Lord, and the eyes of the Lord go back and forth and to and fro throughout the whole earth. There is an all-seeing eye that continually follows the acts of men, leaving them bare before the Judge of heaven. No man can cover his sins and prosper. Instead of fleeing from God, man must flee to God. At the foot of the Cross, his sins will be sent on to judgment, cast into the depths of the sea, removed as far as the east is from the west, and erased from the memory of God.

Sin causes man to flee from God. Ever since Adam and Eve sinned, man has tried to justify himself before God and to cover his sins from the sight of men: "The eyes of them both were opened, and they knew that they were naked; and they sowed fig leaves together, and made themselves aprons. And they heard the voice of the Lord God walking in the garden in the cool of the day: and Adam and his wife hid themselves from the presence of the Lord God amongst the trees of the garden" (Gen. 3:7-8).

Friend, you might successfully hide your infidelity from your wife, your cheating from your employer, your hypocrisy from your pastor, your immorality from your neighbors, but you cannot hide yourself from the omnipresent God. A change of environment will not take you out of the territory of His omnipresence. God is not localized nor confined to a particular locality, for the heaven of heavens cannot contain Him. Heaven is His throne, and the earth is His footstool; and in His own words, "Am I a God at hand, saith the Lord, and not a God afar off? Can any hide himself in secret places that I shall not see him? saith the Lord. Do not I fill heaven and earth? saith the Lord" (Jer. 23:23-24). Or, in the words of the psalmist, "Whither shall I go from thy spirit? or whither shall I flee from thy presence? If I ascend up into heaven, thou art there: if I make my bed in hell, behold, thou art there. If I take the wings of the morning, and dwell in the uttermost parts of the sea; even there shall thy hand lead me, and thy right hand shall hold me" (139:7-10).

III. THE JOURNEY AWAY FROM GOD IS A DOWNWARD JOURNEY

My friend, there is no place on earth where you can escape the presence of God. Notice Jonah got aboard the ship; the Bible says that he paid the fare. A journey away from God is always the most expensive that one can take. It is not the initial fare that is so expensive, but it is the cost of the final trip, for the "wages of sin is death" (Rom. 6:23), or the wages of sin is hell. The journey away from God might seem like an attractive tourist excursion, but it will always leave you broke and penniless. The Prodigal Son ran from his father, but he paid for his trip and made the journey to a far country. The initial cost wasn't much, but his final fare left him penniless. There arose a mighty famine, he spent all, he began to be in want, and he said, "I perish" (Luke 15:17). That is the cost of running from God. Wearied of his constant struggle from the call of God and against the will of God, Jonah fell fast asleep. He was not aware of the danger. He was hardened to the call. Constant and persistent running from God will cause one to lose his spiritual sensitivity and he will become hardened through the deceitfulness of sin. A repeated rejection of God and His message and messengers will soon cause one to become hardened and calloused until his conscious is seared and he is past feeling.

The Bible says, "The whole world lieth in wickedness" (1 John 5:19), which literally means, "The whole world lies in the lap of the Wicked One." Have you repeatedly rejected the call of God until the gospel no longer attracts you?

The shipmaster said to Jonah, "What meanest thou, O sleeper? arise, call upon thy God" (Jonah 1:6). Paul said, "Awake thou that sleepest, and arise from the dead, and Christ shall give thee light" (Eph. 5:14). "Awake to righteousness, and sin not; for some have not the knowledge of God: I speak this to your shame" (1 Cor. 15:34).

Will you hear God calling to you today? The road away from God is a downward road. In the words of Jeremiah 23:12, "Wherefore their way shall be unto them as slippery ways in the darkness: they shall be driven on, and fall therein: for I will bring evil upon them . . . saith the Lord." When one starts the slippery path away from God, he progressively makes his descent and goes downward. Jonah went down to Joppa, he went down into the ship, and finally he said, "I went down to the bottoms of the mountains" (Jonah 2:6).

Oh, my friend, that journey away from God ends at the very bottom, in the pit of corruption and the heart of hell. When the men of the ship realized that the presence of God was causing their difficulty, they were afraid. They cast Jonah overboard. He could not protest, although he had paid the fare for a full trip. Always remember, the devil never gives you your money's worth. Anytime you barter with the devil, he gets the best of the bargain. You'll pay full fare and only get half benefits.

CONCLUSION

There is a beautiful lesson to learn from this story, along with this sordid picture. It not only tells us how Jonah fled, but it also tells us how God followed him. God not only sent the wind to pursue Jonah, but He prepared a fish to receive him when he had to leave the ship: "Now the Lord had prepared a great fish to swallow up Jonah" (Jonah 1:17). "Then Jonah prayed unto the Lord his God out of the fish's belly" (2:1) when he saw that there was no other way of escape. He said, "I am cast out of thy sight; yet I will look again toward thy holy temple" (v. 4). "When my soul fainted within me I remembered the Lord: and my prayer came in unto thee, into thine holy temple" (v. 7). Then he quoted another psalm: "I will pay that that I have vowed. Salvation is of the Lord" (v. 9).

If you are running from God, God is pursuing you. If you have run into a tempest, it could be that this tempest is caused by Almighty God to awaken you from your sleep. There is no place where you can escape the presence of God. Why not reach out and touch God today? Will you let Him become the Master of your life? Will you take Him as your Savior? Don't resist Him any longer. Don't turn Him away; don't run from Him any longer. With outstretched hands, He beckons for you to come to Him. ✞

SPIRITUAL CONDITIONS OF THE LAST DAYS

"This know also, that in the last days perilous times shall come. For men shall be lovers of their own selves, covetous, boasters, proud, blasphemers, disobedient to parents, unthankful, unholy, without natural affection, trucebreakers, false accusers, incontinent, fierce, despisers of those that are good, traitors, heady, highminded, lovers of pleasures more than lovers of God; having a form of godliness, but denying the power thereof: from such turn away" (2 Tim. 3:1-5).

INTRODUCTION

The terms *the last days, latter times, time of the end,* and *the last time* are used throughout the Word of God to indicate a period prior to the coming of the Lord Jesus Christ. The Bible is very clear concerning many things that will happen in the last days. The political and economic conditions of the last days are foretold. The technological and scientific achievements are set forth in no uncertain terms. The moral and spiritual life in the last days is vividly pictured. It would fail me to discuss all of these various phases, but I would like to focus this message on the spiritual conditions of the last days.

The whole current of contemporary history seems to indicate a climax in the near future. The whole world stands in anxiety, harassed by fear, asking the question, "What will happen next?" While our eyes are focused on world conditions, distress of nations, international conflict, political issues, and technological progress, something is happening in the spiritual world of which most people are unaware.

I. A TIME OF APOSTASY

The New Testament declares that there will be a general apostasy in the last days. The Bible says, "Let no man deceive you by any means: for that day shall not come, except there come a falling away first" (2 Thess. 2:3). This apostasy does not mean merely backsliding, for one can stray from Christ and not become apostate. Apostasy means the abandonment of faith: "Now the Spirit speaketh expressly, that in the latter times some shall depart from the faith, giving heed to seducing spirits, and doctrines of devils" (1 Tim. 4:1). This widespread apostasy began, not from an attack from without, but from within. In the theological seminaries and pulpits of our day, the cardinal principles of God's Word have been undermined. The old songs of the blood have been called insensitive, foolish hymns. Church officials have denounced the Virgin Birth, the substitutionary atonement, the bodily resurrection of Jesus Christ, and His second coming. They declare that there is no personal devil and have instituted a moral, ethical religion.

This generation has rationalized faith until it has taken out of the gospel every vital quality and miracle-working power. Deep spirituality has been changed for vague religiousness, without a definite born-again experience with God. Sound doctrine is scoffed at and multitudes of people, who were at one time beaming, glowing Christians, seem to express little or no interest in true religion at all but rather turn their backs upon God. The Bible says, "For the time will come when they will not endure sound doctrine; but after their own lusts shall they heap to themselves teachers, having itching ears; and they shall turn away their ears from the truth, and shall be turned unto fables" (2 Tim. 4:3-4). Christ, in His Mount

Olive Discourse, warned of the deception of these days: "And many false prophets shall rise, and shall deceive many" (Matt. 24:11). The number of false prophets and false religions will increase in the last days.

When churches become spiritually dead, members are starved for spiritual food and they become fertile soil in which false religion can take root. The world is hungering for satisfaction and this is the reason for the growth of false cults in these last days. When men depart from the faith, the Bible says that they will give heed to seducing spirits, or deceiving spirits, and doctrine of devils. Man is incurably religious and the spirit that is within him cries for something to worship. His search for satisfaction has often caused him to be deceived and fall prey to false doctrine. This is the reason that Jesus warned: "Take heed that no man deceive you" (Matt. 24:4). The apostle John wrote, "Many deceivers are entered into the world, who confess not that Jesus Christ is come in the flesh. This is a deceiver and an antichrist" (2 John 1:7). God's Word declares, "But evil men and seducers shall wax worse and worse, deceiving, and being deceived" (2 Tim. 3:13).

The apostle Peter gave this warning about false prophets who deny the blood and the purchase price of Calvary: "But there were false prophets also among the people, even as there shall be false teachers among you, who privily shall bring in damnable heresies, even denying the Lord that bought them, and bring upon themselves swift destruction" (2 Peter 2:1). They are "wells without water, clouds that are carried with a tempest" (v. 17), "raging waves of the sea, foaming out their own shame" (Jude 13), and "sensual, having not the Spirit" (v. 19).

II. AN INCREASE IN FALSE RELIGION

As the time of the end draws nearer, more and more we will see the feverish activity of false religion at work.

Widespread ignorance of God's Word also accounts for the rapid growth of false religions. In this age of intellect and reason when the world is more literate than any period in human history, men are ignorant of the truth. The Word of God says, "This know also, that in the last days perilous times shall come" (2 Tim. 3:1). Men shall be "ever learning, and never able to come to the knowledge of the truth" (v. 7). "And they shall turn away their ears from the truth, and shall be turned unto fables" (4:4).

Listen to the Word of God: "Behold, the days come, saith the Lord God, that I will send a famine in the land, not a famine of bread, nor a thirst for water, but of hearing the words of the Lord" (Amos 8:11). That time of spiritual famine is here. There was a day when the majority of the churches taught the Bible and those who attended the meetings had some background and spiritual knowledge. The Word of God was read and taught in the public schools and the old Book was read around the family altar. This background of scriptural knowledge made it easier for the evangelist to reap a spiritual harvest, but there is a lack of a biblical background among people of the world today, which makes it increasingly more difficult for evangelistic campaigns to be conducted successfully. Instead of the Word of God being preached, taught, read and believed, it is being criticized in schools, pulpits, and colleges and even in the homes. The Word of God upon which our nation was founded has now become an offence to the people. When God's Word becomes an offence to us, a curse rests upon us and we bring all of the plagues and the judgments of God's Book upon us. This, my friend, places us in a precarious condition, for God cannot favor those who willfully deny Him.

The devil has deceived people into believing that some type of religion is better than no religion at all. Therefore, many people have adopted the philosophy that it makes no difference what you believe just so you believe something. Here are two warnings: "Let no man deceive himself" (1 Cor. 3:18); "There is a way which seemeth right unto a man, but the end thereof are the ways of death" (Prov. 14:12). Every individual must have a personal encounter with the Lord Jesus Christ.

Christ has declared that there is only one way. There are not many routes leading to heaven, there is only one route. Jesus Christ said, "I am the way, the truth, and the life: no man cometh unto the Father, but by me" (John 14:6). "Strait is the gate, and narrow is the way, which leadeth unto life, and few there be that find it" (Matt. 7:14). There is "one Lord, one faith, one baptism" (Eph. 4:5). The idea that God has placed many religions and beliefs in the world so that people can believe most anything and live almost any way and still make it to heaven, is but a subtle doctrine of the devil that damns the souls of men. There is only one way, my friend. You must find that way, for anyone who climbs up "some other way, the same is a thief and a robber" (John 10:1).

III. INCREASED FORMALITY OF CHURCHES

Another prevailing condition in these last days is the formality of churches. This is one of the basic difficulties in fundamentalism. Our churches are so cold, lifeless, and dead, the altars are barren. It is true that the churches are filled with activity, but where are these active people on prayer meeting night? It takes a movie, a party, or a social to attract some people to church. This is no doubt what Paul meant when he said, "Having a form of godliness, but denying the power thereof" (2 Tim. 3:5). The form of religion increases, while religion itself becomes more and more powerless. Formality breeds indifference, lukewarmness, and worldliness and is a fertile field in which false religion can grow.

The church at Laodicea is the picture of some of today's

churches. God's charge was that they were "neither cold nor hot" (Rev. 3:16). From all indications it was a progressive church, they were rich and increased in goods, and the testimony of the members was that they had need of nothing. They were organizationally correct, they were making material gains, and had the appearance of success. God looked at this formal church and said, "I will spue thee out of my mouth. . . . Thou art wretched, and miserable, and poor, and blind, and naked" (vv. 16-17).

These are days when successes are determined by material gains, programs, and financial drives. As essential as these things are, they can only serve as vehicles to carry the gospel and when they become anything other than that, they're accursed to us. The forces of formalism have stifled religious conviction, paralyzed the nerve center of the church, and drained men of their compassion for the lost. It has caused churches to relegate to being mere social clubs and service centers rather than great evangelistic centers where men can find the way out of darkness into the marvelous light.

Where there is formalism there is no resistance against worldliness. The world has eaten its way into the church as a cancerous growth and has left the church pale and anemic without energy to resist the things of the world. It is difficult to tell the difference between the church members and the sinners today, if we judge by the way they live. So many church members have given themselves over to almost every form of worldly indulgence until there is no longer a clear line of demarcation between the church and the world. It is no wonder that so many have rebelled from the house of God, and that in many quarters the church no longer has the magnetic drawing power God intended it to have. The church, like Israel, has changed its glory for that which doth not profit. This formality, lukewarmness, and lethargy was set forth in the parable of the ten virgins. Five of them were wise and five were foolish. What was the difference? They all had lamps, they all took their lamps with them, they were all virgins, and they all had the appearance of readiness. But when the cry was made, "Behold, the bridegroom cometh; go ye out to meet him" (Matt. 25:6), it was discovered that the foolish virgins had no oil in their lamps. They had the form but no fire, they had the appearance but no power, and they had the religious exercise but not the reality. The story ends in a sad note: "And while they went to buy, the bridegroom came; and they that were ready went in with him to the marriage: and the door was shut. Afterward came also the other virgins, saying, Lord, Lord, open to us. But he answered and said, Verily I say unto you, I know you not" (vv. 10-12).

CONCLUSION

Could it be possible that you are going through the motions of religion, and living under the shelter of the church? You belong to the church, you are active in the church, and yet you are unprepared to meet Jesus Christ.

I am calling upon you to examine yourself today in the light of the fact that the midnight cry will soon be given and only those who are ready will be admitted to the Marriage Supper of the Lamb. ✞

TAKE TIME TO BE HOLY

"Follow peace with all men, and holiness,
without which no man shall see the Lord"
(Heb. 12:14).

INTRODUCTION

After a very busy day, I settled down in my study to reflect upon the happenings of the day. As I mused upon the busyness of the day, my mind was drawn to the song "Take Time to Be Holy." In my meditation the question that presented itself was "What is holiness?" Does it really take time to be holy? Then I thought, *Holiness is Christlikeness.*

The Scripture says:

- "Be holy; for I am holy" (Lev. 11:44).
- "He that saith he abideth in him ought himself also so to walk, even as he walked" (1 John 2:6).
- "Every man that hath this hope in him purifieth himself, even as he is pure" (3:3).
- "As he is, so are we in this world" (4:17).

While holiness comes as an instantaneous experience, it also carries with it an element of growth:

- "But grow in grace, and in the knowledge of our Lord and Saviour Jesus Christ" (2 Peter 3:18).
- "But speaking the truth in love, may grow up into him in all things, which is the head, even Christ" (Eph. 4:15).

The Word of God speaks of adding Christian graces to our experience:

> And beside this, giving all diligence, add to your faith virtue; and to virtue knowledge; and to knowledge temperance; and to temperance patience; and to patience godliness; and to godliness brotherly kindness; and to brotherly kindness charity. For if these things be in you, and abound, they make you that ye shall neither be barren nor unfruitful in the knowledge of our Lord Jesus Christ (2 Peter 1:5-8).

Not only does God speak of adding Christian graces to our experience but also multiplying them:

- "Mercy unto you, and peace, and love, be multiplied" (Jude 2).
- "And the Lord make you to increase and abound in love one toward another, and toward all men" (1 Thess. 3:12).

I. IT TAKES TIME TO BE HOLY

It does take time for us to reach these spiritual plateaus and peaks in our experience. Many things steal our time and rob us of our times of devotions and consecration. The multiplicity of duties, business cares, family cares, and the demands of these times have stolen our Christian graces. We cannot push in from a work-a-day world and step into His presence and communion. Of course, there is a sense in which we are continually in His presence, because He is omnipresent.

I am speaking here in the sense of entering into the Holy of Holies and having sweet communion with Him. That is His special presence. So many distractions prevent us from reaching the sublime height of holiness God intended for us. The Word of God says, "That ye may attend upon the Lord without distraction" (1 Cor. 7:35). We war against so many things that we must bring into captivity the thoughts in our mind, gird up the loins of our mind, and fight against the straying mind when we approach Almighty God.

The devil is a master of distraction; he manufactures all sorts of distractions to keep us from drawing closer to Calvary. One must continually battle against these distractions like Abraham when he offered his sacrifice to the Lord. The vultures swept down to steal his sacrifice from the altar and Abraham had to drive them back. When we come before God the vultures of hell sweep down upon the altar and endeavor to distract us. We must drive these vultures back in order to have communion with Him.

The church today is filled with so much activity, but very little agony. There are many programs about Christ, but Christ has been left out of the programs. We have been occupied with things that pertain to Christ, but in our busyness we have lost Christ. I would like to ask you the question Christ asked His disciples in the Garden of Gethsemane: "What, could ye not watch with me one hour?" (Matt. 26:40). How long has it been since you spent one hour with your Lord, at His feet and bathed with His glory? Peter, James, and John fell asleep while Jesus Christ was but a stone's throw away, praying passionately. It was not that they could not hear His agony and hear His cries before Almighty God that they went to sleep; but in the midst of this, while He sobbed, they slept. Could it be true that you are asleep today in the midst of these critical times?

II. HOLY PEOPLE ARE PEOPLE OF PRAYER

The Bible says, "But the end of all things is at hand: be ye therefore sober, and watch unto prayer" (1 Peter 4:7). In other words, watch for an opportunity for prayer. The times demand that we seek God's face. Holy men have always been men of prayer. Of John Fletcher, John Wesley said, "He is the holiest man I ever knew." This follows to reason because it is said of John Fletcher that he stained the study walls with the breath of his prayers. Everyone knows John Wesley as a holy man.

Several times I have visited Wesley's chapel on City Road in London, England. I always delight in visiting the house where Wesley spent the last twelve years of his life. I am impressed as I visit the room that Wesley used as a prayer room. In this room, he spent one hour every morning and one hour every night. He had established a habit of prayer. Those who fail to set aside special time for prayer and devotion are seldom, if ever, great men of God. The psalmist said, "I prevented the dawning of the morning, and cried" (119:147). Literally, it means "I arose before the break of day and prayed." Before he could hear the shuffling outside his windows, or the creaking of the carts on their way to the market, or the rabble of the crowd on their way to pedal their wares, he called upon God. And in order for man to be effective in his dealings with men, he must first face God. If he is to have power with man, he must first have power with God. David established the proper habits of devotions.

David said, "My voice shalt thou hear in the morning, O Lord; in the morning will I direct my prayer unto thee, and will look up" (5:3). David was saying, "As sure as morning comes, I will pray and look unto Thee." He had a prayer schedule: "Evening, and morning, and at noon, will I pray, and cry aloud: and he shall hear my voice" (55:17). Not only did David have a prayer schedule, but he had a praise schedule, for he said, "Seven times a day do I praise thee because of thy righteous judgments" (119:164).

Daniel had a schedule of prayer: "He kneeled upon his knees three times a day, and prayed, and gave thanks before his God" (Dan. 6:10). This was the habit that made him a holy man, gave him power over ravenous lions, and brought him safely through the lions' den.

Often Jesus was seen against the background of the rising sun as He agonized in prayer: "And in the morning, rising up a great while before day, he went out, and departed into a solitary place, and there prayed" (Mark 1:35). His form was often seen in the shadow of the night agonizing before God: "And it came to pass in those days, that he went out into a mountain to pray, and continued all night in prayer to God" (Luke 6:12).

III. WAITING ON THE LORD GIVES US STRENGTH FOR HOLINESS

It is waiting before the Lord that gives strength for His holiness. The Word of God says, "Then went king David in, and sat before the Lord" (2 Sam. 7:18). Most of us rush through the day without giving time for communion and devotion to God. We are like the parents of Jesus, going a day's journey supposing Him to be in the company, only to find that at the end of the day He is missing. The parents of Christ left Him for one day, but it took three days to find Him. This is a lesson for all of us to learn, that when we leave Christ out of our lives and fail to contact Him for just one day, it takes time to regain the spiritual strength we lost. If we would be holy, we must wait upon the Lord. The Bible says:

- "Their strength is to sit still" (Isa. 30:7).
- "But they that wait upon the Lord shall renew their strength; they shall mount up with wings as eagles; they shall run, and not be weary; and they shall walk, and not faint" (40:31).
- "Wait on the Lord: be of good courage, and he shall strengthen thine heart: wait, I say, on the Lord" (Ps. 27:14).

To be holy, we must take time to meditate upon Him. Meditation causes the fires of holiness to burn in your heart. The psalmist says, "My heart was hot within me, while I was musing the fire burned" (39:3). There is no place for the world in a burning heart. All the dross has been purged and the heart refined, but it takes time for meditation. One must draw aside from the busy day and tithe his time as did Isaac: "And Isaac went out to meditate in the field at the eventide" (Gen. 24:63). The holy man meditates upon God's Word, for "his delight is in the law of the Lord; and in his law doth he meditate day and night" (Ps. 1:2).

IV. HOLINESS REQUIRES COMMUNION WITH THE LORD

It is the aim of Satan to keep us occupied with earthly things in order to rob us of our holiness. But holiness requires close communion with Christ. The bosom companionship of Peter and John with Christ was reflected in their lives, for the people "took knowledge of them, that they had been with Jesus" (Acts 4:13). Jacob took time to be holy, and after an all-night prayer meeting his holiness was known to all by the change that had been wrought in his life. The greatest testimony to holiness is not a sermon or a testimony, but a life lived in His presence. We must take time to worship. Man must worship something, for man is so made until he must cry out for the supernatural.

Most people have set up idols in their hearts, bow at the shrine of materialism, and there worship. The Bible tells us: "Give unto the Lord the glory due unto his name; worship the Lord in the beauty of holiness" (Ps. 29:2). One cannot worship with a divided mind. Worship requires a singleness of heart and it takes time to close the world out and focus attention on the Lord. We must take time to praise Him. Praise is born out of meditation upon His goodness and appreciation for His benefits. The rush and bustle of these days does not provide for this kind of worship. So we must make the time, as the apostle Paul said: "Redeeming the time, because the days are evil" (Eph. 5:16).

This is what the psalmist did as he looked up in the heavens and said, "The heavens declare the glory of God; and the firmament sheweth his handywork. Day unto day uttereth speech, and night unto night sheweth knowledge" (19:1-2). David's life was a life of continual praise. Everywhere David went he found something about which to praise and magnify God. He shouted with a voice of triumph, he clapped his hands and praised God for all of His wondrous works to the children of men. This should be our attitude, but it takes time to praise God.

CONCLUSION

Don't let Satan rob you of the holiness of God. For here lies the secret of Christian success and power. Ask God now to forgive you for crowding Him to the background and allowing material things to dominate your life. Oh, if God would be given the proper time, this world's ills would be healed and this old world would bow at the feet of Him who loved us and gave Himself for us. Yes, we must take time out of the busy schedules of this life to be holy men and women. The Bible asks us, "Seeing then that all these things shall be dissolved, what manner of persons ought ye to be in all holy conversation and godliness, looking for and hasting unto the coming of the day of God, wherein the heavens being on fire shall be dissolved, and the elements shall melt with fervent heat?" (2 Peter 3:11-12).

"Nevertheless we, according to his promise, look for new heavens and a new earth, wherein dwelleth righteousness. Wherefore, beloved, seeing that ye look for such things, be diligent that ye may be found of him in peace, without spot, and blameless" (vv. 13-14).

In the light of these times, let us take time to be holy. ✞

THE BAPTISM IN THE HOLY GHOST

"I indeed baptize you with water unto repentance: but he that cometh after me is mightier than I, whose shoes I am not worthy to bear: he shall baptize you with the Holy Ghost, and with fire" (Matt. 3:11).

INTRODUCTION

The baptism in the Holy Ghost is a subject about which there has been considerable controversy since the first effusion of the Spirit on the Day of Pentecost. There are various schools of thought as to what the evidence of this experience is and how one may know that he has received it. Some people teach and believe that one receives the baptism in the Holy Ghost at conversion. Another school of thought is that the baptism in the Holy Ghost is the experience of sanctification, or the "second blessing." Still others believe the baptism in the Holy Ghost is an enduement of power for service accompanied by the initial evidence of speaking with other tongues as the Spirit gives utterance. Let us consider each of these in the light of God's Word.

I. SOME BELIEVE WE ARE BAPTIZED IN THE HOLY GHOST AT CONVERSION

The first belief to consider is that we are baptized with the Holy Ghost at conversion. The scripture used to substantiate this doctrine is found in 1 Corinthians 12:13: "For by one Spirit are ye all baptized unto one body, whether we be Jews or Gentiles, whether we be bond or free." This scripture is definitely not talking about the baptism in the Holy Ghost, but the agency of the Holy Ghost in the unification of the body of Christ. It is the office work of the Holy Spirit to weld the body of Jesus Christ together, for we are all members of one body by reason of our association with Jesus Christ. So then this scripture simply means that through the Spirit we are all incorporated into the mystical body of Christ or baptized into one body.

Another scripture used in an effort to prove that one is baptized in the Holy Ghost at conversion is Galatians 3:27: "For as many of you as have been baptized into Christ have put on Christ." No mention is made here of baptism in the Spirit, but a baptism into Christ. The same terminology is used in Romans 6:3-4: "Know ye not, that so many of us as were baptized into Jesus Christ were baptized into his death? Therefore we are buried with him by baptism into death." We also have this statement: "Buried with him in baptism" (Col. 2:12). In dealing with the subject of the baptism in the Holy Ghost, there is one thing that we must understand—and that is that the Word of God speaks of several baptisms.

Each time the word *baptism* is mentioned, we must carefully consider the context in order to properly determine what is meant. The Bible speaks of baptism in water, baptism into the Body, baptism into Christ, the baptism of His death, and the baptism in the Holy Ghost.

- *Baptism in water*: "Go ye therefore, and teach all nations, baptizing them in the name of the Father, and of the Son, and of the Holy Ghost" (Matt. 28:19).
- *Baptism into the Body*: "For by one Spirit are we all baptized into one body" (1 Cor. 12:13).
- *Baptism into Christ*: "For as many of you as have been baptized into Christ have put on Christ" (Gal. 3:27).

- *Baptism of His Death*: "But I have a baptism to be baptized with" (Luke 12:50).
- *Baptism in the Holy Ghost*: "I indeed baptize you with water unto repentance: but he that cometh after me is mightier than I, whose shoes I am not worthy to bear: he shall baptize you with the Holy Ghost, and with fire" (Matt. 3:11).

Some will possibly raise an objection that there is only one baptism, based on Ephesians 4:4-5: "There is one body, and one Spirit, even as ye are called in one hope of your calling; One Lord, one faith, one baptism." Again the context must be considered, for here this scripture is talking of one body, one Spirit, one hope, one Lord, one faith, one baptism, one God and Father. This scripture is also talking about the unity of the body of Christ, and there is one baptism into this Body. This baptism is not the baptism in the Holy Ghost, but it is effected through the agency of the Holy Ghost.

Much of the confusion arises through misunderstanding of the biblical terminology. It is not the contention of Pentecostal believers that all true Christians do not have the Spirit, but the Bible plainly sets forth in Romans 8:9, "Now if any man have not the Spirit of Christ, he is none of his." Therefore, every born-again believer has a portion of Spirit but does not receive the fullness of the Spirit until he is baptized in the Holy Ghost.

According to Galatians 4:6, "God hath sent forth the Spirit of his Son into your hearts, crying, Abba, Father." Every born-again believer has this cry in his heart:

- "Hereby we know that he abideth in us, by the Spirit which he hath given us" (1 John 3:24).
- "Hereby know we that we dwell in him, and he in us, because he hath given us of his Spirit" (4:13).
- "The love of God is shed abroad in our hearts by the Holy Ghost" (Rom. 5:5).

- "For as many as are led by the Spirit of God, they are the sons of God" (8:14).

It is not my purpose to deny that there is a sense in which all born-again believers have the Spirit, for the Spirit is the agency of the new birth: "The wind bloweth where it listeth, and thou hearest the sound thereof, but canst not tell from whence it cometh, and whither it goeth: so is every one that is born of the Spirit" (John 3:8); "Not by works of righteousness which we have done, but according to his mercy he saved us, by the washing of regeneration, and renewing of the Holy Ghost" (Titus 3:5).

My purpose is to show the difference between the new birth, or regeneration, and the baptism in the Holy Ghost. There is a decided difference in the terms *born of the Spirit* and *baptized in the Spirit*. There is one Holy Ghost, but there are diversities of operations according to 1 Corinthians 12:6. The Holy Ghost is a member of the Godhead and was the Creator of the universe: "And the spirit of God moved upon the face of the waters" (Gen. 1:2). "Thou sendest forth thy spirit, they are created: and thou renewest the face of the earth" (Ps. 104:30). "By his spirit he hath garnished the heavens; his hand hath formed the crooked serpent" (Job 26:13). The Holy Spirit had charge of bringing order out of chaos when He brooded over the earth, which "was without form, and void" (Gen. 1:2). The beautiful order of the universe can be attributed to the work of the Holy Spirit. The beauty of the galaxies is the garnishment of the Holy Ghost. The white, fleecy clouds that drift along with a blue background, the twinkling stars, and planets are all the work of the Holy Spirit.

It was through the Spirit that Jesus Christ offered Himself upon Calvary: "Who through the eternal Spirit offered himself without spot to God" (Heb. 9:14). It was the Holy Spirit who had a part in creating man. The Godhead—God the Father, God the Son, and God the Holy Ghost—said,

"Let us make man" (Gen. 1:26). So through the Spirit, man was created. The Spirit convicts of sin, for the Scripture says, "And when he is come, he will reprove the world of sin, and of righteousness, and of judgment" (John 16:8). This is the first act of the Spirit's work in relationship to fallen man.

After a man is convicted and convinced by the Holy Spirit of his sinfulness, He is then a candidate to be born of the Spirit. Jesus said, "Verily, verily, I say unto thee, Except a man be born of water and of the Spirit, he cannot enter into the kingdom of God" (3:5). It is plain to see that as the Spirit was the agent in the creation of the heavens and earth, in the creation of man, in the death of our Lord Jesus Christ, and in the conviction of humanity, so is He the agent in bringing about the new birth in the lives of repentant men and women.

The experience of conversion is for the world—those who are unsaved. The experience of the baptism in the Holy Ghost is for those who have been regenerated by the Spirit of God. Jesus said, "If ye love me, keep my commandments. And I will pray the Father, and he shall give you another Comforter, that he may abide with you for ever; even the Spirit of truth; whom the world cannot receive, because it seeth him not, neither knoweth him: but ye know him; for he dwelleth with you, and shall be in you" (14:15-17). Here Jesus declared that the world cannot receive the baptism in the Holy Ghost. Only those who are already acquainted with the Spirit could receive this glorious experience about which He prophesied.

II. SOME BELIEVE BAPTISM IN THE HOLY GHOST IS A CRISIS EXPERIENCE OF HOLINESS

At this point the second school of thought comes up for consideration, and that is that the baptism in the Holy Ghost is the second blessing—a crisis experience of holiness in the life of believers called *sanctification*. This belief is based on

Romans 15:16: "being sanctified by the Holy Ghost." This is a very prominent belief among holiness groups.

They have been made aware through the Scriptures that there is an experience subsequent to the new birth. Therefore, they contend that the baptism in the Holy Ghost with fire cleanses the inbred sin principle. The close study of the baptism in the Holy Ghost will reveal that this experience does not deal with the sin principle nor does it make one holy. It has to do with spiritual usefulness rather than with the graces of character.

Again, we must recognize that the Holy Spirit is the agent in sanctification and separation, for it is the Holy Spirit who gives power and victory over sin. The baptism in the Holy Ghost is not perfect love or pertaining to a life of perfection, for love is a fruit of the Spirit and is shed abroad in our hearts by the Holy Ghost. And, as the Spirit controls and directs our lives, love is added and multiplied in the Christian's life. Those who waited in the Upper Room for the descent of the Spirit had already experienced great joy: "And he led them out as far as to Bethany, and he lifted up his hands, and blessed them. . . . And they worshipped him, and returned to Jerusalem with great joy" (Luke 24:50, 52). The Bible says, "And the disciples were filled with joy, and with the Holy Ghost" (Acts 13:52). So we see there is not one scriptural reference to call sanctification the baptism in the Holy Ghost. Neither is there any inference that the baptism in the Holy Ghost and sanctification are the one and selfsame experience.

III. BAPTISM IN THE HOLY GHOST IS AN ENDUEMENT WITH POWER

This brings us to the third consideration. That is that the baptism in the Holy Ghost is an experience subsequent to a clean heart, and it is an enduement of power for service with the initial evidence of speaking in other tongues as the Spirit gives utterance. Here are five scriptures that have reference to the baptism in the Holy Ghost that was to be poured out upon those who were believers and living separated lives. Notice the references are to a baptism yet to be and not as yet experienced or bestowed at that particular time.

- "He shall baptize you with the Holy Ghost, and with fire" (Matt. 3:11).
- "He shall baptize you with the Holy Ghost" (Mark 1:8).
- "He shall baptize you with the Holy Ghost and with fire" (Luke 3:16).
- "The same is he which baptizeth with the Holy Ghost" (John 1:33).
- "But ye shall be baptized with the Holy Ghost not many days hence" (Acts 1:5).

The promise of the baptism in the Holy Ghost extends from the appearance of the forerunner, John the Baptist, to the ascension of our Lord.

In the first four scriptures, John the Baptist speaks; in the last scripture, Jesus Christ himself speaks. In all of these scriptures the announcement is prophetic, thus verifying that there was no baptism in the Spirit before the ascension of our Lord. Therefore, the disciples of the Lord Jesus were born-again believers, sanctified through the blood of the cross, but had not as yet received their Holy Spirit baptism. The Holy Ghost was not given, for Jesus was not yet glorified. But Christ had promised that when He ascended on high He would ask the Father to send the Holy Ghost: "I will pray the Father, and he shall give you another Comforter, that he may abide with you for ever" (John 14:16). And the Bible declares, "Therefore being by the right hand of God exalted, and having received of the Father the promise of the Holy Ghost, he hath shed forth this, which ye now see and hear" (Acts 2:33).

The question is asked, "What happens when an individual

receives the baptism in the Holy Ghost?" The doctrine that speaking with other tongues is the initial outward physical evidence of the baptism in the Holy Ghost is based on accumulated evidence that is recorded in the Book of Acts where the believers received this experience. In every case, without exception, there was some outward manifestation that could be seen and heard when the Spirit fell upon them.

The biblical basis of this statement is found in these scriptures: "And they were all filled with the Holy Ghost, and began to speak with other tongues, as the Spirit gave them utterance" (2:4); "While Peter yet spake these words, the Holy Ghost fell on all them which heard the word. And they of the circumcision which believed were astonished, as many as came with Peter, because that on the Gentiles also was poured out the gift of the Holy Ghost. For they heard them speak with tongues, and magnify God" (10:44-46). Peter, in testifying concerning this experience, said that the same thing happened to the people at Cornelius' house that happened to the 120 on the Day of Pentecost: "And as I began to speak, the Holy Ghost fell on them, as on us at the beginning" (11:15). This is conclusive proof that those at Cornelius' house received the identical experience as those on the Day of Pentecost. The evidence was that they had heard them speak with tongues and magnify God.

Another record is given in Acts 19:6: "And when Paul had laid his hands upon them, the Holy Ghost came on them; and they spake with tongues, and prophesied." This record clearly gives speaking with tongues as the evidence of the incoming Holy Ghost. All three of these examples distinctly set forth speaking with tongues as the initial evidence of the baptism in the Holy Ghost.

CONCLUSION

It is suggested by some that the apostle Paul did not speak with tongues when he received his Holy Spirit baptism.

They base this on Acts 9:17: "Brother Saul, the Lord, even Jesus, that appeared unto thee in the way as thou camest, hath sent me, that thou mightest receive thy sight, and be filled with the Holy Ghost." There are some who contend that speaking with other tongues is not the initial evidence on the premise that nothing is mentioned about speaking with tongues in this particular scripture, which refers to Paul's being filled with the Holy Spirit. It might also be well for us to notice that the scripture does not say that Paul was filled with the Holy Ghost on this particular occasion. It merely states that Ananias had been sent that he might receive the Holy Ghost. It is generally believed that this was the time that Paul received the Holy Ghost. There must have been a time that he spoke with tongues, for Paul said, "I thank my God, I speak with tongues more than ye all" (1 Cor. 14:18). Is it not logical that he received this experience when he was baptized with the Holy Ghost?

We have one more biblical example where people were baptized with the Holy Ghost and no specific mention is made of speaking with other tongues. However, it is inferred. A great revival broke out in Samaria. The Scripture says, "Now when the apostles which were at Jerusalem heard that Samaria had received the word of God, they sent unto them Peter and John: Who, when they were come down, prayed for them, that they might receive the Holy Ghost" (Acts 8:14-15). Now notice the next two verses: "(For as yet he was fallen upon none of them: only they were baptized in the name of the Lord Jesus.) Then laid they their hands on them, and they received the Holy Ghost" (vv. 16-17). Notice the Bible terminology, "fallen upon them." What happened at Cornelius' house when the Holy Ghost fell on those who heard the Word? They spoke with tongues. Then is it not logical and feasible that when the Holy Ghost fell on these people they received the same experience? It had to be a manifestation that could be seen, for verse 18 tells us, "And when Simon saw that through laying on of the apostles' hands the Holy Ghost was given, he offered them money." Simon saw some outward evidence. It was not joy, healing, or casting out of unclean spirits that he saw. All these had happened before this particular time. But Simon saw the supernatural manifestation of speaking with other tongues.

My friend, if you have an open heart and you want to receive this blessed experience, bow your head, and pray that God will pour out His Spirit upon you. ✞

THE CRY FROM BENEATH

"There was a certain rich man, which was clothed in purple and fine linen, and fared sumptuously every day: And there was a certain beggar named Lazarus, which was laid at his gate, full of sores, And desiring to be fed with the crumbs which fell from the rich man's table: moreover the dogs came and licked his sores. And it came to pass, that the beggar died, and was carried by the angels into Abraham's bosom: the rich man also died, and was buried; And in hell he lift up his eyes, being in torments, and seeth Abraham afar off, and Lazarus in his bosom. And he cried and said, Father Abraham, have mercy on me, and send Lazarus, that he may dip the tip of his finger in water, and cool my tongue; for I am tormented in this flame" (Luke 16:19-24).

INTRODUCTION

The story of the rich man and Lazarus, as related by Jesus, is one of the most striking stories of the entire Bible. Time and again it has served to awaken the conscience of man. It has been said that they must be fast asleep who are not startled by it. In this story we have a pictorial account of other worlds and a glimpse behind the veil into regions beyond. We hear the conversation of one who has departed this life. We also have the reply of the heavenly Father. We have a cry from beneath—the distresses, cries, and prayers of a man who left God out of his life.

We know very little about the world beneath. No full description is given of hell as there is of heaven. We know that hell is more than a state of being or a condition. It is a literal place. In this story we have the testimony of this man who was confined there, and in his words, it was called a place of torment. We are not left in doubt as to the location of hell:

- "The way of life is above to the wise, that he may depart from hell beneath" (Prov. 15:24).
- "Yet thou shalt be brought down to hell, to the sides of the pit" (Isa. 14:15).
- "And thou, Capernaum, which art exalted unto heaven, shalt be brought down to hell" (Matt. 11:23).
- "Therefore hell hath enlarged herself, and opened her mouth without measure: and their glory, and their multitude, and their pomp, and he that rejoiceth, shall descend into it" (Isa. 5:14).
- "For a fire is kindled in mine anger, and shall burn unto the lowest hell" (Deut. 32:22).

We know there is literal fire in hell, for such terms as *furnace of fire*, *fire and brimstone*, *hellfire*, *unquenchable fire*, *everlasting fire*, and *eternal fire* are used in the Bible to depict hell.

I. A PORTRAIT OF HELL

Here are some scriptures that give a portrait of hell:

- "And shall cast them into the furnace of fire" (Matt. 13:50).
- "Depart from me, ye cursed, into everlasting fire" (25:41).
- "And he shall be tormented with fire and brimstone" (Rev. 14:10).
- "These both were cast alive into a lake of fire burning with brimstone" (19:20).

- "And all liars, shall have their part in the lake which burneth with fire and brimstone" (21:8).

Again, I hear the words of the rich man in hell as he says, "I am tormented in this flame" (Luke 16:24). This is literal fire as we know it. If there should be some doubt in the minds of people about this being literal fire, note what the Bible says: "And the smoke of their torment ascendeth up for ever and ever" (Rev. 14:11). It is literal fire, a fire that produces smoke. Yet, man shall burn forever and ever in this fire. This is the part that the modern man cannot understand. But if God made the bush to burn in the land of Midian and the bush was not consumed (see Ex. 3:2), we must realize that the miracle-working God can prepare a fire to punish the wicked that will not consume them. We know that there is consciousness in hell, for the rich man could see, feel, taste, and hear. It is evident that one has the faculty of memory, for Abraham calls upon the rich man by these words, "Son, remember."

II. PROPER VALUES IN LIFE

Now, let us look at this story which is filled with soul-stirring utterances and warnings. The story is not just an account of two individuals, but represents the state of the righteous and the unrighteous when they depart this life. In this story, Jesus is painting a portrait of the proper values of life. He draws from two extremes: a rich man named Dives, who fared sumptuously and was accustomed to every delicacy of earth to satisfy his appetite and fancy, and on the other hand, a beggar named Lazarus, whose body was covered with sores from malnutrition and his only comfort was from the dogs. But as the story reveals, both of these men went the way of all men of earth. All must face death, regardless of station or status in life, for the Bible says, "There is no man that hath power over the spirit to retain the spirit; neither hath he power in the day of death" (Eccl. 8:8).

"And it came to pass, that the beggar died" (Luke 16:22). Notice the scriptural account does not say that he was buried. He was carried by the angels unto Abraham's bosom. The statement "Abraham's bosom" is used to express the future state of blessedness. The Jewish people sometimes use the term *Garden of Eden*, *Paradise*, or *Throne of Glory*. But in this case the *bosom of Abraham* is used. It carries with it the idea of a great feast of which Abraham was the host. Here the beggar had angels for pallbearers that carried him across the great divide to lie in the bosom of Abraham as the most favored guest at the feast.

The Word of God bears out the fact that when one dies, and he has lived for Christ, he immediately goes to be with the Lord: "We are confident, I say, and willing rather to be absent from the body, and to be present with the Lord" (2 Cor. 5:8). "For I am in a strait betwixt two, having a desire to depart, and to be with Christ; which is far better" (Phil. 1:23). "Then shall the dust return to the earth as it was: and the spirit shall return unto God who gave it" (Eccl. 12:7).

To the thief on the cross who accepted the Lord Jesus Christ, Jesus said, "To day shalt thou be with me in paradise" (Luke 23:43). Numerous scriptures verify the fact that when a Christian dies his spirit goes to be with the Lord while his body rests in the grave until the morning of the resurrection. The Bible says that the rich man also died. His riches could not delay that, nor could they hold him in good standing in the day of death. But unlike the beggar, the rich man "was buried" (16:22). The Scripture continues, "And in hell he lift up his eyes" (v. 23). The word *hell* simply means the unseen world of the dead. It is not the final lake of fire. In the Greek, it is called *Hades*. The final lake of fire is called *Gehenna*; however, it should be noted here that this is not the grave. According to Christ, there is torment there. There are flames of fire there. The wicked man wanted to leave, so it is a world of consciousness. Hades was a place of confinement for the rich man until the day when the Judge of all earth shall call forth the wicked dead to stand before the Great White Throne Judgment. At that time, the sentence will be given and the angels will bind him and cast him in the lake of fire, where he shall burn forever and ever.

Before the resurrection of Jesus Christ, there were two compartments to Hades, upper and lower compartments—the upper compartment for the righteous and the lower compartment for the departed wicked spirits—but when Jesus came forth from the grave and "ascended up on high, he led captivity captive, and gave gifts unto men" (Eph. 4:8). He ascended on high and established Paradise above, and then the Scripture was fulfilled that hell had enlarged herself and opened her mouth without measure.

III. THE CRIES FROM BENEATH

My friend, today I invite you to listen to some cries from beneath. Dives looked across the great gulf that separated him from Lazarus and cried, "Father Abraham, have mercy on me, and send Lazarus, that he may dip the tip of his finger in water, and cool my tongue" (Luke 16:24). The tongue that had tasted the delicacies of earth and had been pleased by the finest of beverages now craved only a drop of water. His tongue had been satisfied and pampered by sumptuous living, and now it seems to suffer most. Those things that one feasts upon on earth and allows the unbridled lusts of his body to engage in will torment him most in hell. There they retain the same appetite, but they will go unsatisfied.

Notice the cry from beneath, "Send Lazarus" (v. 24). He was calling for him to send that poor, putrid beggar with just one drop of water to touch his tongue. He did not ask for a glassful or even a cupful, but just one drop of water. What excruciating pain he must have borne that made him feel he could receive relief from just one drop of water. Lazarus once sat at his gate and would have eaten the crumbs that fell from the rich man's table, but now the rich man wants just one drop from the banquet of Lazarus. What a contrast! The man who was clothed in rags of earth now wears the linen robes of glory. The man who was clothed in purple and fine linen now wears the rags of torment. Now Lazarus sits at the banquet table of glory and feasts from the delicacies of the table of God and eats angel food. The rich man, Dives, becomes the beggar and would be pleased with only a drop of water.

My friend, can you see the contrast of the future state of the righteous and the wicked? Can you see how utterly lost and doomed man will become? That when one, who had all the wealth of this world that he could amass and all that he could ask for, after he had lost it all, wanted but one drop of water! But Lazarus, the beggar for life, will be a prince throughout eternity. And I say to every Christian "that the sufferings of this present time are not worthy to be compared with the glory which shall be revealed in us" (Rom. 8:18). When we shed the rags of this old earth and don the robes of righteousness in the wardrobes of glory, we will then realize that the wicked had their portion in this life but the righteous in the life to come.

Abraham answered the cry of the rich man by saying, "Son, remember" (Luke 16:25). Remember, sinner, that today the devil will rock you to sleep and keep you drugged and doomed by the pleasures of this life. In hell your conscience will no longer be dulled by the pleasures of this world. It will be one of the sharpest pains of your deserved damnation.

Hell is no land of forgetfulness, but a world of pain and everlasting memory. Abraham said, "Thou in thy lifetime receivedst thy good things" (v. 25). In other words, you lived for the world and you received your reward. But the righteous live for the other world and now Lazarus is comforted and the rich man is tormented.

CONCLUSION

The second cry from beneath was, "I pray thee therefore, father, that thou wouldst send him to my father's house: for I have five brethren; that he may testify unto them, lest they also come into this place of torment" (Luke 16:27-28). This was a cry of concern. If we could hear the voices from hell today, they would cry in unison, "Preacher, Christian worker, layman, testify to my relatives and friends, lest they come to this awful place of torment." But Abraham answered the rich man's cry by saying, "They have Moses and the prophets; let them hear them" (v. 29). God put a premium upon the Word.

But then there was another cry from beneath. "Nay, father Abraham: but if one went unto them from the dead, they will repent" (v. 30). The purpose of miracles is not to bring men to repentance; it is through the Word that men have knowledge of God. Therefore, Abraham said, "If they hear not Moses and the prophets, neither will they be persuaded, though one rose from the dead" (v. 31).

My friend, God has given you the Word. The Word reveals that you are lost, that you must repent and believe, that he that believeth and is baptized shall be saved, and he that believeth not shall be damned. Hear these voices from beneath, take warning from them, and repent. In this message you have heard from the unseen regions and the unknown world. You have heard the voice of the damned. Take heed lest this story be reenacted by you. ✟

THE INFLUENCE OF MOTHERS

"When I call to remembrance the unfeigned faith that is in thee, which dwelt first in thy grandmother Lois, and thy mother Eunice; and I am persuaded that in thee also" (2 Tim. 1:5).

INTRODUCTION

Possibly no other person, including the minister and father, wields so much influence in shaping the destiny of this world than does the mother. Many influences play a part in building the character of children, but the nature of a mother's relationship places her in a position of greater responsibility and accountability than anyone else.

Listen to some of the quotations from prominent men of the influence that mothers had upon their lives:

- Napoleon said, "The future destiny of the child is always the work of the mother. Let France have good mothers and she will have good sons."
- Abraham Lincoln said, "All that I am, or hope to be, I owe to my angel mother."
- John Quincy Adams said, "All that I am my mother made me."
- Henry Ward Beecher said, "The mother's heart is a child's schoolroom."

These are the opinions of prominent men concerning the influence of mothers. I ask the mothers listening to me today, what kind of influence are you wielding upon your family? What kind of an influence do you have upon the world, and what kind of society will you bequeath to the next generation? The mother holds the key of the soul. She stamps the coin of character and makes the being that would be savage, but for her gentle cares, a Christian man.

A few years ago an investigation of 1,200 children was made by Columbia University. It was discovered that there is an agreement in character ideals between children and parents closer by far than the agreement of these children with the ideals of other groups with which they are closely associated. The index of the agreement ran like this: 55 percent was parents; 35 percent was playmates; 14 percent was club leaders; and 3 percent was teachers. Of the two parents, the mother's influence was stronger, for the mothers had three hundred times more influence on their children than did the fathers.

I. THERE IS NO LOVE LIKE A MOTHER'S LOVE

For this reason, mothers, you have an unparalleled responsibility. A mother's chief responsibility is to be the homemaker. This is contrary to the pattern of the modern woman, who is striving for status in society, at the sacrifice of home life. One of the first and chief responsibilities is to her children, for the Bible says, "That they may teach the young women to be sober, to love their husbands, to love their children" (Titus 2:4). There is no love on earth like a mother's love. She attends to her children's hurts, forgives their wrongs, and forbears with all patience. No one is quite so understanding, sympathetic, and tender. A child looking for tenderness and love calls upon its mother.

A good example of the care and love of a mother is told in a Bible story: "And when the child was grown, it fell on a day, that he went out to his father to the reapers. And he said unto his father, My head, my head. And he said to a lad, Carry him to his mother" (2 Kings 4:18). The father knew that in an hour of sickness the mother's love was needed. But does this injunction for a mother to love her children mean that there is to be an absence of discipline? God's Word says, "As many as I love, I rebuke and chasten" (Rev. 3:19).

True discipline is a form of love. Discipline is direction, guidance, and instruction. This generation is living in a confused, frustrated, mixed-up, crazy world, and instruction is one of the greatest gifts that could be offered to the children in this day. Proverbs 29:15 says, "A child left to himself bringeth his mother to shame." How many homes have been disgraced simply because parents, through what they called love, failed to restrain their children from evil and damaging influences. In many cases that which is labeled love is merely neglect. Because parents become weary with correction, they submit to the tides of these times and relax their discipline. Discipline seems to be old-fashioned and contrary to much of modern psychology.

For many years parents have followed the behavioral sciences, which philosophy is to let the child do as he pleases—or let him have expression. This philosophy has produced more delinquents and maladjusted children than the old-fashioned methods of discipline based on the Bible. Parents feel if they discipline their children they will frustrate them. It is true that there are frustrations that accompany discipline, but the child is going to face numerous frustrations in life. When a child faces the frustration of discipline and overcomes it, he or she will be better fitted for society.

II. MOTHERS SHOULD DISCIPLINE WITH LOVE

The Bible states that this is God's way of dealing with children; this is God's way of showing love for a child. To pamper a child is to hurt him. "He that spareth his rod hateth his son: but he that loveth him chasteneth him betimes" (Prov. 13:24). This scripture links discipline with love. Parents need not feel guilty about restrictions, rigidness, and discipline simply because their children rebel against it, for most children have a deep-seated appreciation for parents who have enough concern for them to lovingly administer discipline.

The final outcome of such discipline can usually be couched in the words of Solomon: "Her children arise up, and call her blessed" (Prov. 31:28). There is a period in life psychiatrists have chosen to call "the return to the parents." At that time the young person realizes the discipline of mother and father was only a call of love. Most adults listening to me today can remember the time when you thought your mother was a bit old-fashioned. Her requirements for you were too stringent. Her ideas were obsolete, but today you find yourself with some of the same philosophies as that of the old-fashioned mother. That is, if you were fortunate enough to have that kind of a mother.

Young people will test the limits of their parents. The parents must not succumb to the pressure, for to love their children is not to give in to all of their whims and desires, but to guide them and to "bring them up in the nurture and admonition of the Lord" (Eph. 6:4).

III. MOTHERS ARE TO BE "KEEPERS AT HOME"

Another responsibility of the mother as a homemaker is set forth in Titus 2:5: "To be discreet, chaste, keepers at home, good, obedient to their own husbands, that the word of God be not blasphemed." Notice the statement "keepers at home." Someone has said we are living in a different world today, things are different now. The mother of today has been set free from the bondage of the home. It will make of her a better personality. Her time, and in many cases, her education, will not be wasted on the children. This, my friend, is a distorted picture of things. Education, time, and talent is not wasted when a mother is a homemaker or a "keeper at home." These talents better equip the mother to shape and mold the character of her children for a better society.

This new freedom that mothers have assumed, under the guise of progress, is a contributing factor to delinquency and moral breakdown of the young people of our day. American mothers have left their homes for a job in the office and factory with the thought in mind, "I want my children to have the best of everything. I'm going to see that my child has things in life that I could not have."

This is the materialistic concept of this age. Many mothers feel if they are not given this privilege they are being cheated in life, while son and daughter are left to shift for themselves, and to roam the streets at night unattended, undisciplined, and uninstructed. Mother works for enough money to buy a second car, or to have a few days' vacation, or to keep up with the Joneses. Unless economic necessity demands that a woman work outside the home, her first duty is in the home and to her children who are a heritage of the Lord.

This day has produced an entirely different motherhood. Instead of keepers at home, those who are not occupied with public jobs are occupied with social clubs, bridge parties, society, and other functions that take them away from their homes. The modern woman, in a bid for her place in society, in the words of Peter Marshall, has earned the right to become intoxicated, the right to have an alcoholic breath, the right to smoke, and the right to work like a man and to act like a man. It remained for the twentieth century in the name of progress, in the name of tolerance, in the name of broad-mindedness, in the name of freedom, to pull her down from the throne and to make her like a man.

CONCLUSION

It is from the mother that the child acquires materials from which to build a life. Oh, for a return to old-fashioned mothers, old-fashioned ideals, and old-fashioned morality with behavior "as becometh holiness" (Titus 2:3). Oh, for mothers like Jochebed, the mother of Moses, who cared for him and nurtured him in an hour of danger. Oh, for mothers like Hannah, who led Samuel to the Lord, surrounded him with her prayers, and took him to the house of God. Oh, for mothers like Lois and Eunice, who through their constant family devotion and earnest search of the Scriptures, brought salvation to their household (2 Tim. 1:5). Oh, for mothers like the mother of Dewey Talmadge, who when she led the family prayers would say, "Oh, Lord God, I ask not for my children wealth or honor, but I do ask that they all be subjects to thy converting grace." Oh, for mothers like Susanna Wesley, the mother of nineteen children, who through faith and prayers influenced and won her children to God.

Mothers, let me ask you the question Elijah asked the Shunamite woman: "Is it well with thee? is it well with thy husband? is it well with the child?" (2 Kings 4:26). Please answer this question, "Mother, is it well with you?" There is no need for you to expect your children to turn out well if you do not give your soul to the Lord. There is no need for you to lead your children in bedside prayer and require them to say table grace if your life is lived contrary to this principle. Mother, I ask you, "Is it well with your soul?" The next question is, "Is it well with your children?" Every mother will face God for the manner in which she has reared her children. Are you willing to face the Judgment? Have you done everything within your power to win your children to the Lord? Or must you hang your head in remorse over misspent days, months, and years. Mothers, give yourselves unto God that you might change the tide of these times and reestablish the family for God. ✞

THE MIRACLES OF CALVARY

"And there are also many other things which Jesus did, the which, if they should be written every one, I suppose that even the world itself could not contain the books that should be written" (John 21:25).

INTRODUCTION

The entire life of Jesus Christ was a life of miracles. The entrance of Christ into the world through the Virgin Birth was nothing short of a miracle. The public ministry and daily life of the Lord was attended by many miracles. Jesus said, "All power is given unto me in heaven and in earth" (Matt. 28:18). The Bible says He "went about doing good" (Acts 10:38).

Jesus was taken to Golgotha and the place of execution was turned into a mount of miracles. Golgotha, which means "the place of a skull," had been the scene of many crucifixions. Felons, thieves, slaves, criminals, and insurrectionists had died there. But now the sinless Son of God was to be crucified there.

Although Jesus did not perform miracles while hanging on the cross, there were miracles around the cross that fully attested to the divine work done at Calvary. As always, the work of Jesus was approved with mighty signs and miracles. The Bible says, "Jesus of Nazareth, a man approved of God among you by miracles and wonders and signs, which God did by him in the midst of you, as ye yourselves also know" (Acts 2:22). He could have stayed the hands of the angry mob that came for Him in the Garden of Gethsemane. Jesus said to

Peter, "Thinkest thou that I cannot now pray to my Father, and he shall presently give me more than twelve legions of angels? But how then shall the scriptures be fulfilled, that thus it must be?" (Matt. 26:53-54). Christ could have called seventy-two thousand angels to His rescue in Gethsemane, but had He been rescued He would not have been the Son of God, for the Scripture must be fulfilled.

When they cried unto to Him, "If thou be the Son of God, come down from the cross" (27:40), it was within His power to do so, for He said, "No man taketh it from me, but I lay it down of myself. I have power to lay it down, and I have power to take it again" (John 10:18). However, the Bible says, "And as Moses lifted up the serpent in the wilderness, even so must the Son of man be lifted up" (3:14). He could have performed many miracles in the hour of His passion, but He rather chose to follow the Scripture and fulfill the word of the prophets.

I. THE MIRACLE OF DARKNESS AT NOON

God the Father attested to the work done on Calvary by miracles from heaven. The first miracle that accompanied the death scene was a three-hour period of darkness. From noon until three o'clock in the afternoon there was darkness over all the land. The sun, only six hours high, hid its face while the Son of God died. The sun's light was not needed; the Bright and Morning Star from on high was shining. There was no sun needed from the heavens, for the Sun of Righteousness was beaming.

This was the day that had two nights—darkness at a time when the sun shone the brightest, for it was dark at noonday. Those who would try to discount the miracles of Calvary would say that it could have been an eclipse of the sun. But we must remember that this darkness lasted for three hours, too long to have been an eclipse.

Let us also realize that this was a time of the Jewish

Passover that was celebrated during the full moon, when an eclipse would have been impossible. The darkness hid the anguish of God's Son from the eyes of the onlookers. When all forsook Him and fled and God turned His eyes away from Him, He went through the winepress alone, and bore the impressed suffering of the sins of all humankind. In the words of the song "Alas! and Did My Savior Bleed?" by Isaac Watts:

> Well might the sun in darkness hide,
> And shut his glories in,
> When Christ, the mighty Maker, died
> For man the creature's sin.

II. THE MIRACLE OF THE RENT VEIL

When Jesus cried with a loud voice and yielded up His spirit, the second miracle took place. The Scripture says, "And, behold, the veil of the temple was rent in twain from the top to the bottom" (Matt. 27:51). The veil of the Temple separated the Holy Place from the Holy of Holies. This veil was a massive mat of woven linen, trimmed with gold and purple embroidery, sixty feet long and thirty feet wide, and it was a thickness of the palm of the hand. The rending of the veil was by the hand of God. The Bible said it was rent from the top to the bottom, which could not have been the ordinary effect of an earthquake, which would have caused a rending from the bottom to the top.

The Temple itself was not affected and the furnishings in the Temple remained intact. No human hands were responsible for the veil being rent in twain, but the unseen hand of God—that wrote the law on tablets of stone, touched the waters of the Red Sea and rolled them back, and touched the rock in the wilderness—is the hand that touched the tapestry in the Temple and split it from the top to the bottom in order to expose God's glory to all the human race. The rending of the veil was a revelation of mystery hid from the ages. The veil excluded all but the high priest, who entered once a year. The plan of our salvation, which had been veiled, was brought to light in the fullness of time. The glory that was hidden from Moses when he cried, "I beseech thee, shew me thy glory" (Ex. 33:18), was hidden from Aaron as he stood within the veil (Lev. 16:2), and was hidden from David when he asked, "Open thou mine eyes, that I may behold wondrous things out of thy law" (Ps. 119:18) was now available to all. Now the mystery that was kept secret since the world began was made manifest in Christ Jesus through His death on Calvary "by a new and living way, which he hath consecrated for us, through the veil, that is to say, his flesh" (Heb. 10:20).

The rending of this veil was symbolic of the flesh of Jesus Christ that was put upon Calvary, giving all humanity right of way into the Holy of Holies. Now there is a way for the sinners in the Holy of Holies, for the Bible says that the Holy Ghost is signifying that the way to the Holiest of all was not yet made manifest, for as yet the first Tabernacle was still standing: "Having therefore, brethren, boldness to enter into the holiest by the blood of Jesus" (v. 19). The rending of the veil meant the abolishment of the Jewish order and Christ became the end of the law, for the law was our escort to bring us to Christ that we might be justified by faith. Now we have no need for a priest to enter in on our behalf; we need no longer wait for the Day of Atonement, for the purpose of our redemption is made clear through the death of Christ upon Calvary. The mercy seat is exposed and we are brought unto God. Christ is "the way, the truth, and the life" (John 14:6), and the way is open to all of us, so that we may "draw near with a true heart in full assurance of faith" (Heb. 10:22).

III. THE MIRACLE OF THE EARTHQUAKE

Another miracle that attended the death of Christ upon Calvary is the earthquake: "And the earth did quake, and the rocks rent" (Matt. 27:51). The elements were disturbed at His death as well as at His birth. At His birth a new star appeared in the heavens, and now at His death the sun pulled a veil over her face and the earth went into convulsions. The earthquake called attention to the divine work that was taking place at Calvary. He who was dying was the Creator of all things: "All things were made by him; and without him was not any thing made that was made" (John 1:3). While the Creator was hanging upon the cross, the earth was forced to pay royal homage to Him. He who had made the valleys and piled up the mountains, put the sun in its flaming orbit and the stars into their sockets, made doors for the sea, and had the wind in His fist was now dying. Therefore, the earth shook and trembled and the rocks rent and moved out of their places. On Sinai, God used an earthquake to call attention to His law, so is it not fitting that He would use an earthquake to draw attention to the gospel? The earth seemed to cry out against those who were crucifying the Son of God. Their conscience was shaken and they were awakened to His personal divinity, for the Bible says, "Now when the centurion, and they that were with him, watching Jesus, saw the earthquake, and those things that were done, they feared greatly, saying, Truly this was the Son of God" (Matt. 27:54).

Christ was condemned because He said that He was the Son of God, and this to the Jews was the reason for His death: "He hath spoken blasphemy; what further need have we of witnesses? behold, now ye have heard his blasphemy. What think ye? They answered and said, He is guilty of death" (26:65-66). But now the earth was rocking to and fro like a drunkard and they made the confession, "Truly this was the Son of God."

IV. THE MIRACLE OF THE RESURRECTED SAINTS

Two more miracles need to be brought to our attention—the opening of the graves and the resurrection of the saints.

The Bible says, "And the graves were opened; and many bodies of the saints which slept arose, and came out of the graves after his resurrection, and went into the holy city, and appeared unto many" (Matt. 27:52-53). The stone doors of the tombs were split and flung open. The graves were opened but their dead did not awaken and come forth until after Christ's resurrection. The Bible says, "But now is Christ risen from the dead, and become the firstfruits of them that slept" (1 Cor. 15:20). Not all the graves of the earth opened, but the graves of the saints opened. They were opened in preparation for their resurrection with the Lord Jesus Christ.

Notice the supernatural discrimination in the uncovering of these tombs. The saints were to come forth at the shout of the Conqueror, for the unresisting victim had become the irresistible Victor and would show forth the power of redemption. Jesus was taken down from the cross and put in Joseph's newly made tomb. The Rose of Sharon was cut down and planted in Joseph's garden, but on the third day He arose.

CONCLUSION

Because Jesus was triumphant over death, He has made it possible for us to triumph over death: "For as in Adam all die, even so in Christ shall all be made alive" (1 Cor. 15:22). Christ said, "Because I live, ye shall live also" (John 14:19).

My friend, the resurrection of the saints who came out of their graves at the resurrection of Jesus Christ is a pledge of our redemption and our resurrection. The apostle Paul said, "I would not have you to be ignorant, brethren, concerning them which are asleep, that ye sorrow not, even as others which have no hope. For if we believe that Jesus died and rose again, even so them also which sleep in Jesus will God bring with him" (1 Thess. 4:13-14).

He is able to resurrect your soul: "And you hath he

quickened, who were dead in trespasses and sins" (Eph. 2:1). Jesus can give you a spiritual resurrection and you can find true life in Him, for He said, "I am come that they might have life, and that they might have it more abundantly" (John 10:10). ✞

THE PREMILLENNIAL SECOND COMING

"For the Lord himself shall descend from heaven with a shout, with the voice of the archangel, and with the trump of God: and the dead in Christ shall rise first: then we which are alive and remain shall be caught up together with them in the clouds, to meet the Lord in the air: and so shall we ever be with the Lord. Wherefore comfort one another with these words" (1 Thess. 4:16-18).

INTRODUCTION

The second coming of Christ is one of the doctrines of the church, but there is a danger in this merely being a doctrine that we cherish without it affecting the daily life of a Christian. The Christian church today professes a great deal more than it is willing to practice. Our practice must catch up with our preaching. We must become doers of the Word and not hearers only.

In other words, the second coming of the Lord must get hold of us; it must occupy our thought life and provoke us to holiness in our daily life. The person who says that he believes in the second coming of the Lord Jesus Christ and lives a slack, loose, and worldly life only believes in the doctrine theoretically and not in practice.

The proper perspective of the second coming of Jesus will dominate this life. Modern liberal thinking in the area of religion is incompatible with the fundamental doctrine of the premillennial second coming of the Lord Jesus Christ. One cannot believe that Jesus Christ will soon come again and condone the sinful practices of many church members today. The coming of Christ is the hope of the Church and the comfort of God's people for these troubled times.

I. WHAT DOES PREMILLENNIAL MEAN?

Just what is meant by the premillennial second coming of the Lord Jesus Christ? First, let us discuss what is meant by the word *millennial*. The Word of God teaches that there will be an era when righteousness will reign over all the earth and that Jesus Christ will reign in peace. The Bible says, "Of the increase of his government and peace there shall be no end" (Isa. 9:7). This millennial reign is mentioned six times in Revelation 20. It means a period of one thousand years; therefore, this term used for the thousand-year reign of Jesus Christ is used many times by theologians. The word *millennial* means "one thousand"; therefore, the term is used for the thousand-year reign of Christ upon this earth. But what is the relationship of the return of Jesus Christ to this golden age—this period when righteousness shall reign over the earth? There are three theories which are prominent: the premillennial theory, the postmillennial theory, and the amillennial theory.

The postmillennialists believe that this age of righteousness will be brought about by preaching the gospel and that Christ will eventually come at the end of this period to conclude the affairs of earth. The amillennialists believe there will be no period of righteousness whatsoever, no millennial at all. But the Bible teaches that Jesus Christ himself will come before the age of righteousness begins. This is what we mean by the premillennial second coming of the Lord Jesus Christ. The premillennial second coming of Christ is one advent with two events: first, to resurrect the righteous dead and to catch away the living saints to Him in the air; second, to reign on earth for a thousand years. In the first stage of His coming, He appears in midair and the people who are in Christ will be caught up to meet Him. This event will take place before the Tribulation period, for God's church will not go through the wrath that shall be poured out upon the earth—what is called Daniel's Seventieth Week, or the day of God's rebuke.

II. THE CHURCH WILL BE DELIVERED FROM GOD'S WRATH

The Bible tells us that this phase of His coming is to deliver us from the wrath that is to come:

- "And to wait for his Son from heaven, whom he raised from the dead, even Jesus, which delivered us from the wrath to come" (1 Thess. 1:10).

"Watch ye therefore, and pray always, that ye may be accounted worthy to escape all these things that shall come to pass, and to stand before the Son of man" (Luke 21:36).

- "Because thou hast kept the word of my patience, I also will keep thee from the hour of temptation, which shall come upon all the world, to try them that dwell upon the earth" (Rev. 3:10).

God has promised to deliver His church from the hour of temptation and from the indignation that will be poured out during the Tribulation period. Therefore, in the first phase of His coming, Jesus appears in the clouds of glory in a personal bodily appearance. When Jesus comes for the Church, or for the saints of God, He does not come back to the earth but remains in midair for the saints to be caught up with Him. After the seven-year Tribulation period, Jesus returns with the saints to reign on the earth for a thousand years. This meeting of the saints with Christ in the air is called by theologians "the Rapture."

The word *rapture* comes from the Latin word *rapios*,

which means "to snatch away suddenly." This is what Jesus meant when He said, "And if I go and prepare a place for you, I will come again, and receive you unto myself; that where I am, there ye may be also" (John 14:3). This is also what Paul meant in 1 Thessalonians 4:17: "Then we which are alive and remain shall be caught up together with them in the clouds, to meet the Lord in the air." Paul also said in 2 Thessalonians 2:1, "Now we beseech you, brethren, by the coming of our Lord Jesus Christ, and by our gathering together unto him." Notice these statements: "I will . . . receive you unto myself," "caught up together with them in the clouds," and "our gathering together unto him." This is what we mean by the Rapture. The order of this grand and glorious event is set forth so beautifully in 1 Thessalonians 4:15: "we which are alive and remain unto the coming of the Lord shall not prevent them which are asleep." This simply means we who are living when Jesus Christ comes shall not go before them who are dead in Christ.

Now the first thing that shall happen is that the dead in Christ shall rise. They shall come forth from the grave, for the Bible says, "Marvel not at this: for the hour is coming, in the which all that are in the graves shall hear his voice" (John 5:28). "For the Lord himself shall descend from heaven with a shout, with the voice of the archangel, and with the trump of God: and the dead in Christ shall rise first" (1 Thess. 4:16). This shout is a command or an order like that of a captain, and those who were Christians shall respond to this command as did Lazarus when he came forth at the voice of Jesus. They shall come forth in the power of the resurrection. Accompanying this shout or command will be the voice of the archangel and the trump of God. Then following this resurrection will be a transformation, for the Word of God says, "We shall not all sleep, but we shall all be changed, in a moment, in the twinkling of an eye, at the last trump: for the trumpet shall sound, and the dead shall be raised incorruptible, and we shall be changed" (1 Cor. 15:51-52). When the dead in Christ come forth from the graves, the saints of God who are living will experience this glorious transformation and our vile bodies will "be fashioned like unto his glorious body, according to the working whereby he is able even to subdue all things unto himself" (Phil. 3:21).

It was for this day for which Job longed when he said, "All the days of my appointed time will I wait, till my change come" (14:14). With the righteous dead resurrected, the living saints transformed and given bodies fit for heaven and fashioned according to His glorious body, the next thing that happens is a translation. Notice the sequence—resurrection, transformation, translation—"Then we which are alive and remain shall be caught up together with them [the resurrected dead] in the clouds, to meet the Lord in the air: and so shall we ever be with the Lord. Wherefore comfort one another with these words" (1 Thess. 4:17-18).

I am sure that this is a thrill to all of you who are prepared to meet Jesus Christ. For the Bible says, "Unto them that look for him shall he appear the second time without sin unto salvation" (Heb. 9:28).

III. THE REVELATION OF JESUS CHRIST

The second phase of the premillennial second coming of Jesus Christ is called in the Greek *apocalypse*, which means "the unveiling or the revelation." The first phase of His coming is His appearing in the Rapture, and this phase is the unveiling or the revelation of Jesus Christ. When Jesus Christ comes again for His church and meets them in midair, He will not be exposed to the entire world; only the righteous dead shall hear His voice and come forth from the grave. Only those who know His voice because of free pardon of sin will be caught up to meet Him in the air. No eye shall behold Him at that time but the righteous eye.

After the period of God's wrath upon the earth, He will deal with mankind in the Judgment. Jesus Christ will come again, and the person of Christ will be revealed to the entire world and every eye shall see Him: "Behold, he cometh with clouds; and every eye shall see him, and they also which pierced him: and all kindreds of the earth shall wail because of him" (Rev. 1:7). Zechariah 13:6 says, "And one shall say unto him, What are these wounds in thine hands? Then he shall answer, Those with which I was wounded in the house of my friends." In other words, Christ will be revealed to the world when He comes to establish His kingdom upon the earth. When He returns to establish His kingdom, He will be accompanied by the saints of God who were caught up with Him in the Rapture:

- "And the Lord my God shall come, and all the saints with thee" (Zech. 14:5).
- "And Enoch also, the seventh from Adam, prophesied of these, saying, Behold, the Lord cometh with ten thousands of his saints" (Jude 14).
- "When he shall come to be glorified in his saints, and to be admired in all of them that believe (because our testimony among you was believed) in that day" (2 Thess. 1:10).
- "And the armies which were in heaven followed him upon white horses, clothed in fine linen, white and clean" (Rev. 19:14).

Therefore, at His revelation, He comes with the clouds, with power and great glory, to stage a great spiritual conflict, to fight the battle of Armageddon, to overcome the power of the Antichrist, bind the devil, and usher in the golden age of righteousness.

Not only is the revelation of Jesus Christ predicted, but the very place where Jesus Christ will come back again is also predicted. Zechariah prophesied, "And his feet shall stand in that day upon the mount of Olives, which is before Jerusalem on the east, and the mount of Olives shall cleave in the midst thereof toward the east and toward the west, and there shall be a very great valley; and half of the mountain shall remove toward the north, and half of it toward the south" (14:4).

The Mount of Olives where Jesus Christ gave His discourse concerning the time of His coming and the end of the world will be the scene and the backdrop for the momentous event of His return to earth. His coming shall have such a traumatic effect upon nature itself that the Mount of Olives shall actually split in the middle. His coming shall make such an impact upon the earth until the words of Daniel will be fulfilled: "The stone that smote the image became a great mountain, and filled the whole earth" (2:35). This stone is Jesus Christ, the chief cornerstone, and it will destroy and tear down all the kingdoms of the world to pave the way for righteousness. Not only will His revelation make an impact upon nature, but it will make an impact upon all the people of the earth. The Bible says they "shall wail because of him" (Rev. 1:7). It will be a lamentable time for those who have rejected Christ.

One summer while touring Israel and Jordan, I engaged in conversation with the people. I would usually ask the question, "Are you expecting a Messiah to come?" Without exception, the answer of all Jewish people was "Yes, we are looking for Him to come." When I would ask, "Where do you expect Him to appear?" they would say, "On the Mount of Olives."

Throughout Israel there is a spirit of expectancy, looking for the Messiah to come. But the sad picture is that the Messiah came two thousand years ago and they rejected Him. They were not aware that their Messiah had been the Savior of the world for two thousand years now. Neither were they aware that the Messiah—"this same Jesus, which is taken up from you into heaven, shall so come in like manner" (Acts 1:11), as the angels testified. But when they see and realize that they have rejected Him and turned Him away, the Bible says they will wail because of Him.

CONCLUSION

In conclusion, let us notice the manner of this revelation:

> I saw heaven opened, and behold a white horse; and he that sat upon him was called Faithful and True, and in righteousness he doth judge and make war. His eyes were as a flame of fire, and on his head were many crowns; and he had a name written, that no man knew, but he himself. And he was clothed with a vesture dipped in blood: and his name is called The Word of God. And the armies which were in heaven followed him upon white horses, clothed in fine linen, white and clean. And out of his mouth goeth a sharp sword, that with it he should smite the nations: and he shall rule them with a rod of iron (Rev. 19:11-15).

The Bible says, "For as the lightning cometh out of the east, and shineth even unto the west; so shall also the coming of the Son of man be" (Matt. 24:27). When He comes, He will consume the Antichrist with the Spirit of His mouth, He will destroy him with the brightness of His coming, for He is the victorious Lamb, and the kingdoms of the world shall become the kingdoms of the Lord, and He shall reign forever and forever.

You can reign with Christ in His kingdom if you surrender your life to Him and serve Him today. ✞

THE ROAD TO POWER

"And it came to pass, when they were gone over, that Elijah said unto Elisha, Ask what I shall do for thee, before I be taken away from thee. And Elisha said, I pray thee, let a double portion of thy spirit be upon me" (2 Kings 2:9).

INTRODUCTION

Out of an obscure background, suddenly Elijah appeared on the scene in Bible history. Although he was a man of like passions as we are, his conduct and miracles soon distinguished him as a stalwart giant for God. At his command the heavens became as brass and the clouds closed their doors so that it did not rain for the space of three and a half years. Likewise, when the occasion demanded it, he called down fire out of heaven. After being tormented by Jezebel for his firm stand against the prophets of Baal, he resorted to Mount Horeb, where God spoke to him in a still small voice. When he departed from the Mount he found Elisha the son of Shaphat plowing in the fields with a yoke of oxen. As Elijah passed by this young plowboy, he cast his mantle of camel's hair upon him. This mantle was a symbol of God's presence, and immediately Elisha left the yoke of oxen and ran after Elijah.

He entreated Elijah to allow him to bid farewell to his mother and father and follow him. But Elijah said, "Go back again: for what have I done to thee?" (1 Kings 19:20).

Elijah was aware of what he had done to this young man, but he wanted an expression from Elisha as to why he desired to follow him. Elisha arose and went after Elijah and ministered unto him.

In Elisha's quest for power, there are three things that were prominent: (1) persistence; (2) desire; and (3) self-emptying.

I. ELISHA'S PERSISTENCE TO RECEIVE A DOUBLE PORTION

For eight years Elisha followed in the footsteps of Elijah, he beheld the miracles he performed and ministered unto him. He was not satisfied with merely a touch of the mantle, but he diligently pursued him for a double portion of the Spirit of God. He had felt a touch of this Spirit the first day he came in contact with the mantle. I sincerely believe that no man who is genuinely born of God can be fully satisfied until he has received a double portion of the Spirit that he felt when he received Jesus Christ.

Evidently, it was common knowledge that Elijah was to be transported to glory without seeing death. This was intimated by Obadiah when he met Elijah while looking for pasture for Ahab's cattle (see 1 Kings 18:12). This was also intimated by the conversation of the sons of the prophets at Bethel and Jericho (see 2 Kings 2:3-5).

Elijah was the second man in history to take this mysterious route to heaven. Enoch was the first, having preceded him many years before: "And Enoch walked with God: and he was not; for God took him" (Gen. 5:24). "And it came to pass, when the Lord would take up Elijah into heaven by a whirlwind, that Elijah went with Elisha from Gilgal" (2 Kings 2:1). But try as he would, he could not discourage Elisha from following after him. Three times—at Gilgal, Bethel, and Jericho—Elijah entreated his companion to leave him, but three times Elisha replied, "As the Lord liveth, and as thy soul liveth, I will not leave thee" (v. 6). It seems that Elijah was obliged to yield to the persistence of Elisha. No doubt it was a thrilling experience for Elisha to go to Gilgal, for at *Gilgal*, which means "a rolling away," he must have seen the twelve stones that were a memorial of the children of Israel's crossing of the Jordan River on dry ground. But to remain at Gilgal was to live in the past.

Many Christians are doing this today; they have lost the freshness of their experience and live in the memories of a once-bright Christian life. Those who stop at Gilgal do not have God's best. From Gilgal, they departed to *Bethel*, which means "the house of God." Every man who is searching for a deeper experience with God will have his heart close to the house of God. As David said, "I was glad when they said unto me, Let us go into the house of the Lord" (Ps. 122:1). Even some of the sons of the prophets and the theological students endeavored to discourage Elisha by saying, "Knowest thou that the Lord will take away thy master from thy head to day?" (2 Kings 2:5). His only answer was, "Yea, I know it; hold ye your peace" (v. 5). He seemed to say, "Regardless of what happens, I am hungry for a deeper experience."

They departed from Bethel and went to Jericho. *Jericho* means "a pleasant place." Again the entreating of Elijah and the seminary students could not turn Elisha back. Why should one stop short of the fullness of the Spirit? Why not go all the way with God? As Jacob of old, Elisha seemed to say, "I will not let thee go, except thou bless me" (Gen. 32:26). Jacob had travailed in prayer, and his name was changed from "a deceiver and supplanter" to *Israel*, which means "prince of a nation." Although, Jacob's thigh was smitten by the angel and was out of joint, afterward when he would haltingly walk, all who looked upon him knew by his walk that he had been touched of God.

It can be detected in the walk of a man that he has been

touched by Almighty God or if he has a double portion of the Spirit. The apostle Paul said, "If we live in the Spirit, let us also walk in the Spirit" (Gal. 5:25). Few prophets are willing to pay the full price for power. While the Scripture records, "And they two [Elijah and Elisha] went on" (2 Kings 2:6), the next verse tells us "fifty men of the sons of the prophets went, and stood to view afar off" (v. 7). They were interested onlookers, but only Elijah and Elisha went on. We have many, whom I term Pentecostal spectators, who stand to view afar off these days. They are not hostile to the experience of power, yet they do not go on with God. Like these fifty students, they want to witness something supernatural and miraculous, yet they keep their distance. They will not pay the price.

The Bible says, "And they two [Elijah and Elisha] stood by Jordan" (v. 7). *Jordan* means "the river of God," and the two that stood by the river are indicative of those who stand when the times get hard. The waters parted before these two men of God, and the Scripture records that they two went over. There is no obstacle that can stand in the way of a man who is in pursuit of more power with God.

II. ELISHA'S DESIRE FOR A DOUBLE PORTION

Now, let us notice the desire of Elisha for this double portion: "And it came to pass, when they were gone over, that Elijah said unto Elisha, Ask what I shall do for thee, before I be taken away from thee. And Elisha said, I pray thee, let a double portion of thy spirit be upon me" (2 Kings 2:9). Oh, what desire, what yearning, what longing was in his heart! It is well to notice the desire of Elisha was not for material things to consume upon his own lusts. He coveted earnestly a double portion of the Spirit. This was preeminent in his desire. All other things must become secondary to your desire if you would attain God's best. As the psalmist said, "One thing have I desired of the Lord, that will I seek after" (27:4). The double portion was the oldest son's portion–the portion of an heir. Jacob favored his son Joseph by giving him a double portion. Job received a double portion after his sore trial. Our Pentecostal heritage is a double portion of the Holy Spirit.

The crying need in the Church today is an all-consuming desire for the fullness of the Spirit among its members. There is no substitute for old-time power. "Blessed are they which do hunger and thirst after righteousness: for they shall be filled" (Matt. 5:6).

Elijah told Elisha that he had asked a hard thing. Nevertheless, if Elisha saw him when he was taken up, his request would be granted. This meant that Elisha must be constantly looking up and be expectant. Any man who receives the fullness of the Spirit of God must expect God's Spirit.

Though Jordan had divided before these two men, "they still went on" (2 Kings 2:11). The men who stand by Jordan and go over and still go on are those who will not be denied God's best. As they walked along there appeared a chariot of fire and horses of fire; the two prophets were separated, and Elijah went up by a whirlwind into heaven and Elisha saw it. His desire, plus his vision, had purchased for him the much-longed-for power. Elisha's quest for power was about to reach a climax.

III. ELISHA'S PREPARATION FOR A DOUBLE PORTION

Now, we come to Elisha's self-emptying and his preparation for the fullness of the Spirit. He rent his own clothes into pieces and took up the mantle that fell from Elijah. In order to be clothed upon by the Spirit of God, we must rend the vestments of our own flesh—our self-righteousness—as Isaiah said, "All our righteousnesses are as filthy rags" (64:6). The garments of God can be worn only by those who will rend their own garments. The way to power is the road to self-denial. Jesus said, "If any man will come after me, let him deny himself" (Matt. 16:24).

Oh, that God would send a cloak of His power to clothe

the naked church of our day. Elisha did not try to tailor Elijah's garment to fit his own fancy, as some would have done in this day. There are those who would try to trim and cut down the Pentecostal garment to fit their own fancies, but God set a pattern at Pentecost and everyone who is to succeed must cut his life according to this pattern. There is no bargain-counter experience. No undersized garment will suffice; nothing will substitute for the power of God. Elisha took the mantle of Elijah and made his way to the bank of Jordan. He did not advertise nor publicize that he had received a double portion, but he wanted to have the manifestation as the evidence of the experience. He smote the waters with the mantle and asked, "Where is the Lord God of Elijah?" (2 Kings 2:14). The waters rolled back and he passed through on dry ground. His experience was evident to others and the sons of the prophets began to exclaim, "The spirit of Elijah doth rest on Elisha" (v. 15). Elijah was gone, but Elijah's God still existed. When the waters parted, it was a divine ratification that God had fulfilled Elisha's desire. He had received a double portion of the Spirit, for he did twice as many miracles as Elijah. When the world sees the manifestation of the power of God, they will begin to make inquiry. But the church will not be heard for her much speaking, but for her power.

Many of these sons of the prophets urged Elisha to allow them to go and search for Elijah (see v. 16). The characteristic of those who stand afar off from God's operation is that they have their eyes blinded by doubt and unbelief and fail to see the infallible works of God as they really are. Though there was doubt in the minds of these students, there was no doubt in the mind of Elisha, for God had translated his spiritual father. Yet, Elisha permitted them to go. After three days' search, they returned knowing that God makes no mistakes. Realizing the power of Elijah was resting upon Elisha, they began to resort to him with their needs.

CONCLUSION

My friend, the people of the world will turn to the church with their needs when they realize there is power in the church to meet their needs. Healings and mighty miracles always follow a double portion of the Spirit.

Who today will cry for the mantle of Elijah? Who today will say, "I am a candidate for a double portion of the Spirit of God"? This should be the cry of all Christendom.

If you are hungry for a double portion of the Spirit, call out to God in prayer now. He wants you to "be filled with the Spirit" (Eph. 5:18). ✞

THE VALUE OF OUR TRIALS

"My brethren, count it all joy when ye fall into divers temptations; knowing this, that the trying of your faith worketh patience" (James 1:2-3).

INTRODUCTION

Not until a Christian understands the purpose and value of the trials of life will he enjoy the Christian experience. Christians through the ages have asked the question "Why do Christians suffer? Why do they have to bear afflictions and trials?" Some Christians have despaired because they did not know the answer and could not understand. When Job was going through the darkest trial of his life and could not understand why, he cried out, "Shew me wherefore thou contendest with me" (10:2).

Job was perfect and upright before God, yet God permitted him to be tried as few men in history have been tried. Satan was permitted to attack Job to prove his uprightness and fidelity to God and to show the benefits of trust even in times of adversity. Job was a wealthy man, yet he was stripped of his houses, lands, cattle, and was even bereft of his ten children. He was so completely stripped of the things of this life until he cried out, "Naked came I out of my mother's womb, and naked shall I return thither: the Lord gave, and the Lord hath taken away; blessed be the name of the Lord" (1:21). His friends turned against him in the hour of need. His own wife told him to curse God and die at a time when his sickness was almost unbearable.

Job had the proper attitude in the time of his trial. He didn't allow the trials to cause him to lose sight of God. He cried out, "But he knoweth the way that I take: when he hath tried me, I shall come forth as gold" (23:10). The reason that he could have this attitude in trial is revealed in these verses: "My foot hath held his steps, his way have I kept, and not declined. Neither have I gone back from the commandment of his lips; I have esteemed the words of his mouth more than my necessary food" (vv. 11-12). This was the premise upon which Job could claim the presence of God in the time of trial. This was the thing that gave him courage.

The Word of God says, "Take, my brethren, the prophets, who have spoken in the name of the Lord, for an example of suffering affliction, and of patience. Behold, we count them happy which endure. Ye have heard of the patience of Job, and have seen the end of the Lord; that the Lord is very pitiful, and of tender mercy" (James 5:10-11).

My friend, the attitude you have during your affliction will determine to a great extent the value and the profit of your trial. Through the trial of Job, he saw himself and his imperfections, but he also beheld the glory of the Lord. He saw his weakness, but he beheld the strength of God. When Job had successfully braved his trial, the Word of God says that "the Lord gave Job twice as much as he had before. . . . So the Lord blessed the latter end of Job more than his beginning" (Job 42:10, 12).

I. NOT ALL TRIALS COME FROM GOD

We must first understand that not all trials come from God. There are three sources from which trials come. First, the trials of Christians may come from God; second, they may come from Satan through the permissive will of God; or third, they may be the result of our own faults, failures, or sin. The word *trial* means "an experiment or search made upon a man by some affliction to prove the value and strength of his faith." In order to know how to cope with the trial, we must understand the source. If we are buffeted for our own faults, we can but plead the mercy of God for our help and strength. The Bible says, "For what glory is it, if, when ye be buffeted for your faults, ye shall take it patiently? but if, when ye do well, and suffer for it, ye take it patiently, this is acceptable with God" (1 Peter 2:20). Many of the trials which Christians have to bear are brought upon them through neglect and failure. There is little profit to be derived from trials of this nature, for they have not been sent from God for a purpose.

God tries or tests us that He might bring out the best that is in us. The Bible said that God tempted Abraham, which means that He put Abraham to the test or He tried Abraham. It was this trial of Abraham's faith that caused him to be classified as the friend of God and the father of the faithful. The fiery trial of the believer is part of his spiritual development and it awakens in him latent powers that nothing else could do. One has only to look back upon some of the trials of his life to realize that these were some of the greatest moments of his Christian experience and they did more to bring him to the measure of the stature of the fullness of Christ than the mountain-peak moments of seeming victory.

II. TRIALS CAN BE PROVIDENTIAL

Paul considered the trials of his past as providential arrangement in his life. He said, "But I would ye should understand, brethren, that the things which happened unto me have fallen out rather unto the furtherance of the gospel; so that my bonds in Christ are manifest in all the palace, and in all other places" (Phil. 1:12-13). Trials are an appointment of God's people and they should not affect us or move us, for God has so ordered them. First Thessalonians 3:3 says, "That no man should be moved by these afflictions: for yourselves know that we are appointed thereunto." A Christian can better bear his trials when he realizes that God does not send us a trial until we are prepared to bear it. One person has said that trials are God's vote of confidence in us. So then, instead of despairing in our trials, let us glory in our trials. James said, "My brethren, count it all joy when ye fall into divers temptations; knowing this, that the trying of your faith worketh patience" (1:2-3).

How many Christians sympathize with themselves and feel that the trials through which they are going are greater than anyone else has to bear. The Bible says, "Beloved, think it not strange concerning the fiery trial which is to try you, as though some strange thing happened unto you: But rejoice, inasmuch as ye are partakers of Christ's sufferings; that, when his glory shall be revealed, ye may be glad also with exceeding joy" (1 Peter 4:12-13). This scripture literally reads, "Stop thinking it a thing alien to you." These Christians to whom Peter was talking thought that Christians were not supposed to suffer and they were undergoing something that was unjust.

Christianity does not mean immunity to suffering and trial, for the Word of God says, "Yea, and all that will live godly in Christ Jesus shall suffer persecution" (2 Tim. 3:12). If we are to be identified with the Lord Jesus Christ, we must suffer. We are partakers of Christ's suffering. The early disciples were happy to suffer for Christ: "And they departed from the presence of the council, rejoicing that they were counted worthy to suffer shame for his name" (Acts 5:41). The apostle Paul said, "There hath no temptation taken you but such as is common to man: but God is faithful, who will not suffer you to be tempted above that ye are able; but will with the temptation also make a way to escape, that ye may be able to bear it" (1 Cor. 10:13). These things are all common in the eyes of God and common to all humanity. Because God has taken others through them, He will not leave you nor forsake you! We must bear in mind that nothing happens by chance to the Christian. Even these trials for righteousness' sake are within His plan. We must bear in our bodies the marks of the Lord Jesus Christ. As the song says:

Must Jesus bear the cross alone
And all the world go free?
No, there's a cross for ev'ry one.
And there's a cross for me.
Must I be carried to the skies,
On flowery beds of ease,
While others fought to win the prize,
And sailed through bloody seas?

I read a story one time of a mother and her daughter who were to be drowned if they did not deny Jesus Christ. The persecutors took the mother out into the water and made the daughter look upon her as they held her under the water. Her tormentor asked her the question, "What do you see?" Instead of seeing her mother drowning as her tormentor thought she would see, she said, "I see Jesus." In our trials we need to take assurance from what the Word says about trials:

- "In the world ye shall have tribulation: but be of good cheer; I have overcome the world" (John 16:33).
- "Marvel not, my brethren, if the world hate you" (1 John 3:13).
- "For consider him that endured such contradiction of sinners against himself, lest ye be wearied and faint in your minds. Ye have not yet resisted unto blood, striving against sin" (Heb. 12:3-4).

Notice the statement in the above verse: "Consider him." Consider His trials, afflictions, and sufferings and then realize that He is our example and in order to be identified with Him we must be crucified with Him.

III. TRIALS ARE A TEST OF CHARACTER

Trials are a test of character, and those Christians whom

God uses to the greatest extent are usually tried more than others. There is an adage that says, "We must be ground between the millstones of suffering before we can be bread for the multitude." Notice some of the biblical examples:

- The stoning, scourging, imprisonment, beatings, shipwrecks, privations, and other difficulties through which Paul went helped to make him what he was.
- Joseph's trial in Pharaoh's dungeon was a graduate course in patience that brought him to the presidency of Egypt.
- The utter despair of Job and the trials through which he went made his tongue the pen of a ready writer, and through him we have the beautiful piece of literature called the Book of Job.
- The trial of Abraham on Mount Moriah when God called on him to give his son Isaac was the supreme test that made him the father of the faithful.

When the Christian comes to realize that this world is not his portion and the sufferings of this present time are not worthy to be compared with the glory that shall be revealed in us, then he can have the right outlook on life. God did not promise Christians that they would not have burdens, but He said that He would make our burdens light. He did not say that we would not bear a yoke, but He said that He would make the yoke easy. He did not say that we would not have cares, but He said to cast all of those cares on Him, for He cares for us. He did not say that we would not have afflictions, but He did say that our light afflictions which are but for a moment worketh for us a far more and exceeding, eternal weight of glory. "Many are the afflictions of the righteous: but the Lord delivereth him out of them all" (Ps. 34:19).

IV. SOME TRIALS ARE DISCIPLINARY

Sometimes our trials are disciplinary trials. God allows trials to come our way to bring us into conformity with the image of His Son, for the Scripture says, "For whom the Lord loveth he chasteneth, and scourgeth every son whom he receiveth" (Heb. 12:6). If your trial is one of discipline from God, thank Him for it. The Word of God says, "Happy is the man whom God correcteth" (Job 5:17). If you have neglected your prayer life or failed in any portion of your Christian experience, God often sends trials upon you to bring you back to His side. Isaiah said, "Lord, in trouble have they visited thee, they poured out a prayer when thy chastening was upon them" (Isa. 26:16). There are many lessons to be learned in the school of trial. David learned a lesson of obedience, for he said, "Before I was afflicted I went astray: but now have I kept thy word" (Ps. 119:67).

Your afflictions, misfortunes, and disadvantages God has often used as instruments of mercy to awaken you and turn you from your straying. So, my Christian friend, your attitude in time of trial should be the same as Paul: "Most gladly therefore will I rather glory in my infirmities, that the power of Christ may rest upon me. Therefore I take pleasure in infirmities" (2 Cor. 12:9-10).

Now we have the value of our trials: first, God is glorified on our behalf (1 Peter 4:12-16); second, they produce praise, honor, and glory at the appearing of Jesus Christ (1:7); third, they are a test of character (Job 23:10; James 1:2-3); fourth, they prepare us for the greater tasks in life; fifth, they identify us with Christ (1 Peter 4:13); sixth, they prove us and humble us (Deut. 8:2); seventh, they work out patience in our lives (Rom. 5:3); eighth, they are for our profit; and ninth, they yield a peaceable fruit of righteousness (Heb. 12:11) and are more precious than gold that perisheth (1 Peter 1:7).

CONCLUSION

God has put a high premium upon the trials of a Christian, and if you are going through some special trial at this time, receive comfort from this scripture: "Fear thou not; for I am with thee: be not dismayed; for I am thy God: I will strengthen thee; yea, I will help thee; yea, I will uphold thee with the right hand of my righteousness" (Isa. 41:10). Put your trust in Him today. If you are languishing on a bed of sickness, if you are going through what seems to be an unbearable trial, or if you are going through the valley of the shadow, remember He knows your way.

Right now, as I come to the close of this message, you can receive anything you need from God. If you want physical healing, if you want spiritual healing, or if you are having domestic difficulty, financial troubles, or whatever it may be, I recommend the One who will "supply all your need according to his riches in glory by Christ Jesus" (Phil. 4:19). ✞

THE WAY OUT

"Commit thy way unto the Lord; trust also in him; and he shall bring it to pass" (Ps. 37:5).

INTRODUCTION

This is an era of stress and strain. It is a time of fear, confusion, frustration, and complexities. Men are harassed by fear and cast down by anxieties. Such great pressures have been brought to bear upon this present generation until men are going to pieces and this civilization is literally coming apart at the seams. One psychologist, after viewing an alarming number of mental cases, said that psychosis is the stepchild of modern civilization. This generation with its intellectual and scientific progress and its moral decay has produced a frustrated society. Modern pressures of complex living have produced worry, anxiety, and fear. The modern gadgets and push-button controls, devised to make life more comfortable for man, have failed in their purpose. These external luxuries cannot satisfy the aching void of the human soul, for "life is more than meat, and the body is more than raiment" (Luke 12:23).

Mankind has endeavored to achieve peace by human efforts, but when faith is centered in anything outside of God, we are destined to failure. God is the only One who can give balance to life; and when He is left out of the arrangements, there is no balance, thus no peace. Anxious man, in pursuit of the necessities of life, has overlooked the main necessity. Jesus Christ warned us against becoming so anxious and worried about the creature comforts that we lose vision of the mainstream of life. He said:

> Why take ye thought for raiment? Consider the lilies of the field, how they grow; they toil not, neither do they spin: And yet I say unto you, that even Solomon in all his glory was not arrayed like one of these. Wherefore, if God so clothe the grass of the field, which to day is, and to morrow is cast into the oven, shall he not much more clothe you, O ye of little faith? Therefore take no thought, saying, What shall we eat? or, What shall we drink? or, Wherewithal shall we be clothed? . . . for your heavenly Father knoweth that ye have need of all these things (Matt. 6:28-32).

Christ is not telling us to be shiftless, but is warning us about making majors out of minors and giving preeminence to secondary things of life. He said in verse 33, "But seek ye first the kingdom of God, and his righteousness; and all these things shall be added unto you." When you are right with Christ everything else will come into focus. You need no longer worry or fear for all is in His hands.

I. SALVATION IS OF THE LORD

The dilemma of this generation is that men are trying to settle their own problems; they are going to the wrong source for aid. They have created their problems and now they are trying to cure them. The main reason that man does not receive cure for his ills is that he does not realize that "salvation is of the Lord" (Jonah 2:9). Man has resorted to psychiatrists and physicians, who are making a definite contribution to society; but his basic needs are beyond the reach of the psychiatrist or the physician. Psychiatrists in some cases can render relief to the human mind and physicians can operate on the body, but "salvation is of the Lord." Only God has the cure.

A young man came to my office needing counsel. In the course of conversation, I discovered that he had bitterness and malice in his heart and it was warping his entire personality. He told me he had several counseling sessions endeavoring to rid him of this plague. His counselor told him that it might take two and even three years to be freed from this plague. I told him that he could be relieved instantaneously through the Lord Jesus Christ. You can be relieved of the thing that plagues you so even now. Christ said, "I am the way" (John 14:6). He is the way out of difficulty. He is the way out of trouble. He is the way out of worry. He is the way out of anxiety. And, most of all, he is the way out of sin. He is our escape.

Christ does more than deal with symptoms—He is the cure for human ills. The psychiatrist can diagnose cases, but Christ can cure them. Most of the difficulties that men are having today are caused from sin in the human heart, and it is impossible for anyone to remove fear, anxiety, or any other frustration until one first gives his life into the hands of Christ. This is the reason Christ said, "Come unto me, all ye that labour and are heavy laden, and I will give you rest" (Matt. 11:28). This is the reason Peter said, "Lord, to whom shall we go? thou hast the words of eternal life" (John 6:68). He is the source of all satisfaction and there is no permanent lasting satisfaction outside of Him. David said, "I will lift up mine eyes unto the hills, from whence cometh my help. My help cometh from the Lord, which made heaven and earth" (Ps. 121:1-2).

Human problems are so complex that men are looking for complex answers and solutions. It is difficult for them to realize that the solution is simple, uncomplicated, and uninvolved. In fact, the solution to your problems is so simple that many of you overlook it because of its simplicity. The Word of God says, "Casting all your care upon him; for he careth for you" (1 Peter 5:7). It is just as simple as that. God can deliver you from your phobias, fears, and complexes; but you will have to let Him do it His way and follow His pattern. He has the blueprint for your life.

II. ACCEPT CHRIST AS YOUR SAVIOR

If you want deliverance you must first accept Christ as your personal Savior. Say with the psalmist:

- "The Lord is my shepherd; I shall not want" (23:1).
- "The Lord is my light and my salvation; whom shall I fear? the Lord is the strength of my life; of whom shall I be afraid?" (27:1).
- "God is the strength of my heart, and my portion for ever" (73:26).
- "He is my refuge and my fortress: my God; in Him will I trust" (91:2).

Or say, like in other scriptures:

- "My beloved is mine, and I am his" (Song 2:16).
- "God is my salvation; I will trust, and not be afraid: for the Lord Jehovah is my strength and my song; he also is become my salvation" (Isa. 12:2).

Christ has promised to come into human hearts and take up His abode. In the words of Paul: "That Christ may dwell in your hearts by faith" (Eph. 3:17). Therefore, you must not merely give intellectual assent to Christ, but you must believe on Him to the extent that you will risk Him with your life. You must be reckless in your abandon to Him in order to receive true satisfaction. You are probably saying, "Yes, this all sounds good, but how can it come to my life? How can it come to pass?" Here is a simple solution found in Psalm 37:5: "Commit thy way unto the Lord; trust also in him; and he shall bring it to pass." In committing ourselves to Him, there are some things that must be denied, renounced, and forsaken. This is what Christ meant when He said the following:

- "So likewise, whosoever he be of you that forsaketh not all that he hath, he cannot be my disciple" (Luke 14:33).

- "He that loveth father or mother more than me is not worthy of me" (Matt. 10:37).
- "If any man will come after me, let him deny himself, and take up his cross, and follow me" (16:24).

Committal involves complete renunciation, and there can be no true deliverance without absolute renunciation. You must lay every "darling Isaac" on the altar, give up every "beloved Benjamin," and not spare "Agag." Anything short of this type of surrender is halfhearted. In the words of Isaac Watts' hymn, "When I Survey the Wondrous Cross":

> When I survey the wondrous cross
> On which the Prince of glory died,
> My richest gain I count but loss,
> And pour contempt on all my pride.
>
> Forbid it, Lord, that I should boast,
> Save in the death of Christ my God!
> All the vain things that charm me most,
> I sacrifice them to His blood.

This is our response to His sacrifice upon Calvary. "Jesus paid it all, / All to Him I owe." "Take my life, and let it be / Consecrated, Lord, to Thee." Present your body (that is the physical), present your heart (that is the emotional), present your mind (that is the intellectual), and present your will (that is the volitional). Make that first step and say, "All I have—my possessions; all I am—my personality; all I hope to be—my plans and projects—I commit to thee." This is the life the apostle Paul experienced: "I know whom I have believed, and am persuaded that he is able to keep that which I have committed unto him against that day" (2 Tim. 1:12). This is the reason Paul was able to say, "For to me to live is Christ, and to die is gain" (Phil. 1:21). Everything had been committed into the hands of Christ. This is the point at which many people fail. If one will not make this step, he cannot make the other steps.

III. YOU MUST TRUST THE LORD

The same scripture that tells us to commit our way to the Lord says, "Trust also in him" (Ps. 37:5). God calls upon you to put your trust not in a creed, not in a minister, nor a system, but in Him who is "the way, the truth, and the life" (John 14:6).

Jesus said:

- "I am the light of the world: he that followeth me shall not walk in darkness, but shall have the light of life" (8:12).
- "I am the good shepherd: the good shepherd giveth his life for the sheep" (10:11).
- "I am the resurrection, and the life: he that believeth in me, though he were dead, yet shall he live" (11:25).

And the apostle John said, "He that hath the Son hath life; and he that hath not the Son of God hath not life" (1 John 5:12).

Oh, how simple it is! All He is asking you to do is to take Him. It is all of grace through faith. You receive Christ into your heart by faith: "But as many as received him, to them gave he power to become the sons of God, even to them that believe on his name" (John 1:12).

After you have done your part, the next step is God's. Notice again the scripture in Psalm 37:5: "Commit thy way unto the Lord; trust also in him; and he shall bring it to pass." It is God's promise that when we have complied with His pattern, "He shall bring it to pass." Our part in salvation is committal or surrender, which involves repentance, confession, forsaking, and renunciation of sin. After this step, we must believe on the Lord Jesus Christ. The Word of God says, "Believe on the Lord Jesus Christ, and thou shalt be saved, and thy house" (Acts 16:31), and "Whosoever believeth that Jesus is the Christ is born of God" (1 John 5:1). Then God's part is to keep His promise and impart to you new life.

CONCLUSION

Will you accept Jesus Christ and commit your life to Him today? You can only have peace with God through faith in Jesus Christ. This is your way out of your problems and difficulties. This is freedom from your anxiety. This is the way to courageous living in this hour of uncertainty. This is the way to cancel your fears and frustrations, for when you take Christ with you, nothing will be too terrible to face or too hard to endure. Will you accept Him now as your personal Savior? ✞

WHY YOUR PRAYERS ARE NOT ANSWERED

"But your iniquities have separated between you and your God, and your sins have hid his face from you, that he will not hear" (Isa. 59:2).

INTRODUCTION

Prayer is the most powerful weapon in the hands of humankind. In fact, prayer has a limitless power. That God answers prayer is an indisputable fact. God is a prayer-answering God. The Bible says, "O thou that hearest prayer, unto thee shall all flesh come" (Ps. 65:2). Man is invited to pray to God and is promised an answer. Jesus said, "Ask, and it shall be given you; seek, and ye shall find; knock, and it shall be opened unto you" (Matt. 7:7).

Prayer is the breath of the human soul. It is the nerve that moves the muscles of divine omnipotence. Prayer is the cost of Pentecost. It is the cry of the human soul for communion with God. God has made many glorious promises to the human race concerning the answer of prayer:

- "If ye abide in me, and my words abide in you, ye shall ask what ye will, and it shall be done unto you" (John 15:7).
- "Therefore I say unto you, What things soever ye desire, when ye pray, believe that ye receive them, and ye shall have them" (Mark 11:24).
- "And whatsoever ye shall ask in my name, that will

I do, that the Father may be glorified in the Son. If ye shall ask any thing in my name, I will do it" (John 14:13-14).

- "And whatsoever we ask, we receive of him, because we keep his commandments, and do those things that are pleasing in his sight" (1 John 3:22).
- "And this is the confidence that we have in him, that, if we ask any thing according to his will, he heareth us: And if we know that he hear us, whatsoever we ask, we know that we have the petitions that we desired of him" (5:14-15).

In the light of these precious promises, why doesn't God answer your prayer when you pray? I hear the complaint, "I believe in God, but nothing ever happens when I pray." Is your prayer a meaningless ritual, a mechanical practice, and words of vain repetition prayed without expectation? Is your prayer without life and reality? Is it a mere form without force? There must be some reason why your prayers are not answered. The Bible is replete not only with promises to them who pray, but with answers to prayer. All about us we can hear testimonies of persons who know the reality of answered prayer. The conditions of answered prayer must be met before God's promises can be fulfilled. The Scripture says, "And if we know that he hear us, whatsoever we ask, we know that we have the petitions that we desired of him" (v. 15).

I. DOUBT IS A DETERRENT TO ANSWERED PRAYER

How can we know that He hears us? Doubt is one of the greatest deterrents to answered prayer. God demands that we put our full trust and dependence in Him: "Commit thy ways unto the Lord; trust also in him; and he shall bring it to pass" (Ps. 37:5). To doubt or to question His Word is to show the lack of confidence in God. A man who wavers and doubts need not expect anything from the Lord. The

Scripture says, "If any of you lack wisdom, let him ask of God, that giveth to all men liberally, and upbraideth not; and it shall be given him. But let him ask in faith, nothing wavering. For he that wavereth is like a wave of the sea driven with the wind and tossed. For let not that man think that he shall receive any thing of the Lord" (James 1:5-7).

Prayer is the key that opens the door to God, but faith is the hand that turns the key. It is the prayer of faith that produces results: "And the prayer of faith shall save the sick, and the Lord shall raise him up" (5:15). Faith is essential in prayer. When anyone comes to God, he must come in faith, for "without faith it is impossible to please him: for he that cometh to God must believe that he is, and that he is a rewarder of them that diligently seek him" (Heb. 11:6). Faith is the unseen hand that reaches into the throne room of heaven and brings back the answer to our prayers.

How many prayers are merely lip service—prayers read from a book that never come from the heart—vain repetitions repeated over and over as a meaningless ritual? Of such, the Bible says, "Forasmuch as this people draw near me with their mouth, and with their lips do honour me, but have removed their heart far from me" (Isa. 29:13).

One cannot believe for an answer to prayer when he knows his heart is out of tune and contact with God. The Word of God tells us, "The eyes of the Lord are upon the righteous, and his ears are open unto their cry" (Ps. 34:15). The ears of God are closed to those who cannot pray in faith. When an individual knows that his heart is not right with God, he has no right to expect an answer to prayer. All of his praying is in vain.

The individual who prays in faith prays with a spirit of expectancy. He prays with upturned face and outstretched hands waiting for an evidence of things not seen and a substance of things hoped for. I marvel at the unbelief of believers in this day. God's Word has spoken, but they make so many excuses for unanswered prayer. It is time that the church of our day takes an introspective look and the members examine their hearts to determine why God's promises are not fulfilled through their prayers.

II. ANSWERED PRAYERS ARE DEPENDENT UPON ABIDING IN CHRIST

Jesus said, "If ye abide in me, and my words abide in you, ye shall ask what ye will, and it shall be done unto you" (John 15:7). It is useless to pray if we do not abide–if we do not continue in His Word. The Word must be kept in our hearts, for the Word is the basis for our prayer. The Bible says, "He that turneth away his ear from hearing the law, even his prayer shall be abomination" (Prov. 28:9).

The Word of God must not merely be kept in our memory, but it must become part and parcel of our lives, for "faith cometh by hearing, and hearing by the word of God" (Rom. 10:17). It is impossible to approach God without faith, and this faith must be stimulated through the Word of God. One cannot read the Bible and meditate upon the Word of God for long without praying, for the Word drives man to his knees.

The Word of God contains the revealed will of God. The Scripture has told us that if we ask anything according to His will, we shall have it. Therefore, in order to know His will concerning us, we must delight in the Word of God. The neglect of God's Word in this generation is largely responsible for the lack of prayer and for the lack of confidence in prayer. When men neglect the Book, they neglect the demands of the Book. If you have been having difficulty in your prayer life, turn back to the Bible, for you will not read and meditate upon it long until prayer will return to your bosom. When you abide in Him and His words abide in you, you can ask what you will and it shall be done. This is God's Word and God cannot lie. Examine yourself to see if you are abiding in Him.

Many prayers are not answered for the lack of obedience to God's Word. The apostle John said, "And whatsoever we ask, we receive of him, because we keep his commandments, and do those things that are pleasing in his sight" (1 John 3:22). Obedience is better than sacrifice. It is a definite requirement for answered prayer. If there are things you know to do and have failed to do them, remember that an answer to prayer hinges on doing those things that are pleasing in His sight. "If you know these things, happy are ye if ye do them" (John 13:17). Disobedience has stayed the hand of God and withheld your answer, for "no good thing will he withhold from them that walk uprightly" (Ps. 84:11).

III. SOME PRAYERS ARE NOT ACCORDING TO GOD'S WILL

Other prayers are not answered because man does not pray according to the will of God. The Word of God teaches, "This is the confidence that we have in him, that, if we ask any thing according to his will, he heareth us" (1 John 5:14).

The will of God is no secret. Every individual can know God's will. The Word of God says, "Wherefore be ye not unwise, but understanding what the will of the Lord is" (Eph. 5:17). This is sometimes difficult for us because our own wills enter into the picture. It is difficult for us to submit our will to the will of the heavenly Father. We are so bent on receiving what we personally desire until we cannot determine God's will. Like Elijah on Mount Horeb, we look for God in the earthquake, the fire, the storm; but when we get completely out of self, in the quietness of our own secret prayer chamber we can hear the still small voice of the Lord. Oh, why is it that we struggle in our own strength with our own stubborn rebellious wills when God is waiting to do His will in our lives? Some Christians use this point as an excuse for a spiritual lethargy and spiritual laziness. When an answer to prayer does not come, their excuse is that it wasn't God's will. One should search the motives of his heart and be sure that he is not excusing himself. To be resigned to the will of God is one of the most glorious experiences of power that a Christian can receive.

The Gethsemane cry—"Nevertheless not my will, but thine, be done" (Luke 22:42)—requires agonizing prayer and consecration. God does not always choose to answer your prayer in the manner you expect. Here is where our commitment to God's divine will is so essential to the success of a victorious Christian life. This was the place to which Paul came when he prayed twice to be delivered from his thorn in the flesh. When his personal desire was not answered, he was willing to submit himself to the answer of God: "My grace is sufficient for thee" (2 Cor. 12:9). God answered the prayer of the apostle Paul, but not in the way he expected. He did not answer his prayer by removing the thorn in the flesh; but He answered his prayer by giving him grace to bear the thorn. Oh, may the will of God be worked out in all of our lives!

IV. PRAYERS CAN BE UNANSWERED BECAUSE OF SELFISH MOTIVES

Other prayers are hindered because of the selfish motive behind them. The Scripture says, "Ye ask, and receive not, because ye ask amiss, that ye may consume it upon your lusts" (James 4:3). In this case, prayer is not answered because of the lack of a proper motive. If one prays simply for the ratification of self and for his own pleasure, the Bible says that we "ask amiss." The motive of our prayers will determine whether or not they are answered. The motive must be pure. How many times have persons prayed for perfectly legitimate things, but it was a prayer amiss simply because they wanted these things for their own personal glory? Jesus said, "And whatsoever ye shall ask in my name, that will I do, that the Father may be glorified in the Son" (John 14:13). This is the real purpose in prayer—to glorify the Father. If the Father cannot be glorified in your prayer and through your prayer, then you need to reevaluate the purpose.

Sin always hinders prayer. In fact, no man can contact God for an answer to prayer with sin in his life, as the following scriptures reveal: "If I regard iniquity in my heart, the Lord will not hear me" (Ps. 66:18); "But your iniquities have separated between you and your God, and your sins have hid his face from you, that he will not hear" (Isa. 59:2).

If one has sin in his life, he cries to God in vain until that sin is confessed. If you cannot get a prayer through to God, why not cry out, "Search me, O God, and know my heart: try me, and know my thoughts: and see if there be any wicked way in me, and lead me in the way everlasting" (Ps. 139:23-24). Sin has always blighted and separated man from God. You cannot expect an answer with sin in your heart. "Son of man, these men have set up their idols in their heart, and put the stumblingblock of their iniquity before their face: should I be enquired of at all by them?" (Ezek. 14:3).

Whatever the sin in your heart is, it must be removed. Whether it is an idol you have set up in your heart, bitterness against a brother, or an unforgiving spirit, sin must be removed. Prayer is answered on the basis that our sins are forgiven. Anyone who is nursing a grudge or has allowed the gall of bitterness to remain in his heart or who has anything against a brother cannot expect God to answer his prayer: "And when ye stand praying, forgive, if ye have ought against any: that your Father also which is in heaven may forgive you your trespasses" (Mark 11:25). We cannot expect forgiveness until we have forgiven others. We cannot expect God to answer prayer until sin is removed.

V. PRAYERS CAN BE UNANSWERED BECAUSE OF WRONG RELATIONSHIPS

The last reason for unanswered prayer is a common one

that few people recognize. The Bible says, "Likewise, ye husbands, dwell with them according to knowledge, giving honour unto the wife, as unto the weaker vessel, and as being heirs together of the grace of life; that your prayers be not hindered" (1 Peter 3:7). This scripture verifies the fact that a wrong relationship between husband and wife is a hindrance to prayer. Unkindness, quarrelsomeness, bickering, sharpness, and ungovernable temper in the home—all of these things will break contact with God. Therefore, it is necessary that our hearts be right before Him when we approach His throne. If we know that He hears us, then we know that we have the petition that we ask of Him, and we can know that he hears us when we have been obedient to His Word.

CONCLUSION

Do you feel as if your prayers are not being answered? Does it seem that your prayers are not getting through to God? You can be assured that God hears every prayer, but some of the things discussed in the message may be hindering your prayers.

Why not call out to God now and ask His forgiveness for anything that may be hindering an answer to your prayers. It is God's will to answer your prayers, for Jesus said, "But rather seek ye the kingdom of God; and all these things shall be added unto you. Fear not, little flock; for it is your Father's good pleasure to give you the kingdom" (Luke 12:31-32). ✞

WITH CHRIST IN THE STORM

"Now it came to pass on a certain day, that he went into a ship with his disciples: and he said unto them, Let us go over unto the other side of the lake. And they launched forth. But as they sailed he fell asleep: and there came down a storm of wind on the lake; and they were filled with water, and were in jeopardy. And they came to him, and awoke him, saying, Master, master, we perish. Then he arose, and rebuked the wind and the raging of the water: and they ceased, and there was a calm. And he said unto them, Where is your faith? And they being afraid wondered, saying one to another, What manner of man is this! for he commandeth even the winds and water, and they obey him" (Luke 8:22-25).

INTRODUCTION

Much of the ministry of the Lord Jesus Christ was centered around the Sea of Galilee. I have had the privilege of visiting Galilee twice. Each time the waters were calm, peaceful, and placid. But the Sea of Galilee, being about 682 feet below sea level, is subject to violent storms, though it is a small body of water about six miles wide at its widest point and approximately twelve miles long. The cool winds rushing down through the mountain gorges and meeting the warm air of Galilee cause sudden and severe storms.

This is what happened to Jesus and His disciples when they were crossing to the other side of the sea. Christ had ordered His disciples to enter into the ship and cross over to the other side.

It is wonderful to notice that Jesus Christ does not command us to go anywhere that He will not go with us. The Scripture states that He went into a ship with His disciples. They that obey Christ's orders may assure themselves of His continual presence. His presence is predicated upon obedience to His command. He commanded His disciples to go and teach all nations to observe all things He had commanded. Then he said, "Lo, I am with you alway, even unto the end of the world" (Matt. 28:20). He has only promised to be with those who are obedient to His command. The Scripture says, "Let your conversation be without covetousness; and be content with such things as ye have: for he hath said, I will never leave thee, nor forsake thee" (Heb. 13:5). We can venture anywhere if Christ accompanies us.

I. NO STORM IS TOO SEVERE FOR CHRIST TO TAKE US THROUGH

No storm of life is so severe that Christ cannot take us safely through. God has promised, "When thou passest through the waters, I will be with thee; and through the rivers, they shall not overflow thee" (Isa. 43:2). If we have taken Christ with us into the boat, we can be assured of His timeless presence through every raging storm of life. The Word of God says, "The sea is his, and he made it" (Ps. 95:5). Those who put to sea with Christ must place implicit trust in Him, for though they put to sea in a calm, they must be ready for the storm.

All of life is filled with storms as well as calms. This is a lesson that is difficult for young Christians to learn, and sometimes difficult for mature Christians to remember. Christ did not promise us that cares would not present themselves, but the Bible assures us of His care for us: "Casting all your care upon him; for he careth for you" (1 Peter 5:7).

Christ did not say that burdens would not come, but He said, "My yoke is easy, and my burden is light" (Matt. 11:30). He did not say that afflictions would not present themselves, but His Word says, "For our light affliction, which is but for a moment, worketh for us a far more exceeding and eternal weight of glory" (2 Cor. 4:17).

II. EXPERIENCING A STORM DOES NOT MEAN THAT CHRIST HAS LEFT US

A storm in our Christian experience is no indication that Christ has left us. A Christian's life is filled with persecutions, afflictions, sacrifices, burdens, and difficulties. We must remember that the devil is the god of this world—the prince of power of the air—and it is he who causes many of the storms of life that come upon us. In verse 23 of our text, the Bible says, "And there came down a storm of wind on the lake." But the Bible says that Christ was asleep in the storm.

As long as Christ was on the ship, there was no danger of sinking. This is a simple lesson that we all must learn. We cannot fall as long as Christ is our captain. We cannot go down as long as Christ is on board. It matters not what goes on around us; if we have perfect repose in Him, it cannot affect us. This is the reason His Word says, "Do not fret or have any anxiety about anything, but in every circumstance and in everything, by prayer and petition (definite requests), with thanksgiving, continue to make your wants known to God. And God's peace . . . which transcends all understanding shall garrison and mount guard over your hearts and minds in Christ Jesus" (Phil. 4:6-7 Amp.).

As an old familiar song tells us:

O what peace we often forfeit,
O what needless pain we bear,
All because we do not carry,
Everything to God in prayer!

The disciples began to panic because they had forgotten the simplicity of faith, confidence, and trust. We panic because we fail to remember His promises and to put our faith in His Word. His disciples failed to realize the Bible says that it is God "who layeth the beams of his chambers in the waters: who maketh the clouds his chariot: who walketh upon the wings of the wind (Ps. 104:3). The Bible asks, "Who hath measured the waters in the hollow of his hand, and meted out heaven with the span, and comprehended the dust of the earth in a measure, and weighed the mountains in scales, and the hills in a balance?" (Isa. 40:12). "It is he that sitteth upon the circle of the earth, and the inhabitants thereof are as grasshoppers; that stretcheth out the heavens as a curtain, and spreadeth them out as a tent to dwell in" (v. 22). "Behold, the nations are as a drop of a bucket, and are counted as the small dust of the balance: behold, he taketh up the isles as a very little thing" (v. 15).

Then Isaiah calls upon us to lift up our eyes with these words: "Lift up your eyes on high, and behold who hath created these things, that bringeth out their host by number: he calleth them all by names by the greatness of his might, for that he is strong in power; not one faileth" (v. 26).

III. THE DISCIPLES LOOKED AT THE STORM, NOT CHRIST

The disciples panicked because they looked at the storm and not to Christ. It would be good for us Christians to learn that our experience with Christ is not something that goes on round about us but something that goes on inside of us, and all things will work to the glory of God in the end. The only way to dispel fear and anxiety is to throw ourselves unconditionally and unreservedly upon Him and leave the results in His hands.

This was not an ordinary storm, for these fishermen had braved many storms on the Sea of Galilee. The Bible says the water was raging, the boat was filled with water, and they were in jeopardy. What a consolation to know that in the most severe storms of life God is present to help: "God is our refuge and strength, a very present help in trouble" (Ps. 46:1). When the severe storms of testing come our way, we should allow these storms to drive us deeper into the heart of God instead of allowing the forked lightning, claps of thunder, and rolling clouds to frighten us. Look full into His wonderful face and He will give peace in the midst of the storm.

The disciples cried, "Master, master, we perish" (Luke 8:24). But I repeat, they could not perish as long as Christ was on board the ship. As long as you keep Christ as your companion, He will keep you from all harm.

The Bible says, "Then he arose" (v. 24). Christ always arises in times of distress and difficulty. He arises to meet the needs of His people. He rebuked the wind and the raging of the water and immediately they ceased. The storm left as suddenly as it had come. It is evident that this storm was caused by the prince of the power of the air, who had raised these winds by permission of God. Thus, Jesus rebuked the wind and the raging of the water. Though the Enemy is the prince of the power of the air, Christ, the Prince of Peace, has power over him.

The Scripture says, "And there was a calm" (v. 24). There is always a calm when Christ rises up. Regardless of how many storms beat upon His people, there will always be a calm that follows. It is the business of the Lord to lay storms and to bring calm to His people: "He maketh the storm a calm, so that the waves thereof are still. Then are they glad because they be quiet; so he bringeth them unto their desired haven" (Ps. 107:29-30); "[God] stilleth the noise of the seas, the noise of their waves, and the tumult of the people" (65:7); "Thou rulest the raging of the sea: when the waves thereof arise, thou stillest them" (89:9).

CONCLUSION

As a Christian, we have no guarantee of perpetual calm. When storms come, it does not mean that Christ has left us. The storms should not affect our experience in Him. This is when our experience is put to the test and personal trust in a personal Savior becomes a reality.

Jesus Christ rebuked His disciples for their inordinate fear. He said, "Where is your faith?" (Luke 8:25). This is the question I would like to ask many Christians who are faltering and falling by the wayside under the stress of these times. Where is your faith? Wherefore do you doubt? Why should you allow the petty difficulties of life and the stresses of these times to inundate your experience? If Christ is with you, you cannot sink. You have the consolation that He will go with you always. As the psalmist said, "Yea, though I walk through the valley of the shadow of death, I will fear no evil: for thou art with me" (23:4).

Sinner, is your life one continual storm? The Bible says, "But the wicked are like the troubled sea, when it cannot rest, whose waters cast up mire and dirt. There is no peace, saith my God, to the wicked" (Isa. 57:20-21). If in your breast there is one continual raging, heaving storm, listen to the words of Jesus: "Peace I leave with you, my peace I give unto you: not as the world giveth, give I unto you. Let not your heart be troubled, neither let it be afraid" (John 14:27). Friend, I am not talking about an outward peace or a temporary peace; but I am talking about a peace that is inward—that war, turmoil, and turbulence cannot disturb. If everything around you goes to pieces and everything in life seems to go into reverse, this peace cannot be disturbed.

This is the peace that I am recommending to you. This peace is not a pact, an armistice, or a contract, but this peace is the Man Jesus. Make your acquaintance with Jesus today and you will find Him to be the peace that passes all understanding—the peace that nothing in the world can disturb. ✞